SAVING
☒ the erring
☒ the church
☒ our families
☒ ourselves

A Study of Church Discipline

Donnie V. Rader

2018 One Stone Press.
All rights reserved. No part of this book may be reproduced in any form without written permission of the publisher.

Published by:
One Stone Press
979 Lovers Lane
Bowling Green, KY 42103

Printed in the United States of America

ISBN: 978-1-941422-27-4

Supplemental Materials Available:
➢ Answer Key
➢ Downloadable PDF
➢ Power Point Slides

www.onestone.com

CONTENTS

1	What Is Discipline?	5
2	Personal Offenses	15
3	Public Offenses	23
4	The Forgotten and Misunderstood Command	31
5	The Purpose of Withdrawing and From Whom Should We Withdraw?	37
6	The Case at Corinth (Part 1)	45
7	The Case at Corinth (Part 2)	53
8	The Case at Thessalonica	61
9	How to Treat Those Disfellowshipped	71
10	Does It Apply to Family?	79
11	Can We Withdraw from the Withdrawn?	87
12	Procedure for Withdrawal	97
13	Objections and Questions about Withdrawing	103

What Is Discipline?

Lesson 1

Church discipline is an effort to save the erring, save the church, save our families, and save ourselves. If we love God, care about the erring, and want to save our families and ourselves, surely, we would want to follow God's plan for saving the erring! That should be true no matter what our thinking may be, and no matter how difficult or painful the process may be.

Church discipline is an emotionally charged subject because close friends and family are often involved. Furthermore, some of the requirements of discipline are hard. In fact, they are downright painful! Much like the marriage, divorce, and remarriage issues, emotions regarding church discipline can easily overshadow knowledge.

As with all issues, we must begin with the understanding that God's way works and is best. The word of God is our only standard (1 Pet. 4:11; Col. 3:17). Our difficulty in applying the principles of church discipline comes down to a matter of faith.

"Church discipline," to most, means "withdrawing" from an unfaithful member. Our objective in this first lesson is to see that "discipline" is much broader and should be practiced far more often than withdrawing. Additionally, we shall see that discipline is necessary for all areas of life.

The Necessity of Discipline

When there is no penalty or consequence for a continual violation of the law, there is no respect for the law itself or the lawgiver.

Discipline is essential to all areas of life (where there is association by common purpose). This is true in work, home, military, and church. In each of these areas, three principles are present. (1) There must be laws, rules, or policies. How can players play a game of sports without some rules? How can administrators have a school without some rules? Society must have laws (Rom. 13:1-7). (2) There must be instruction of the laws, rules, or policies. The school must instruct the students regarding the rules. The company must instruct the employees regarding the policies. The parents must instruct children regarding the rules of the house. (3) There must be some penalty or consequence for violation of the rules. The student gets detention. The criminal is arrested. The player is penalized or ejected from the game. The worker is fired. The private is court-martialed. These same three principles apply to the church.

Without discipline, there would be utter chaos (cf. 1 Cor. 14:33). Imagine a home where the kids do what they want; a game where the players make their own rules or the military where no one is in command. Without discipline, there is no instruction, no training, no correction, no improving, and everyone does what he desires (cf. Judges 21:25).

Discipline is necessary within self. We must have self-discipline or self-control (2 Pet. 1:6; 1 Cor. 9:26-27). If every member of a church practiced self-discipline, there would be little or no need for corrective discipline.

The fact that God tells us to discipline says it is necessary. God expects parents to discipline in the home (Prov. 13:24). The inspired word gives instruction and correction (2 Tim. 3:16-17). The unruly are to be warned (1 Thess. 5:14). We are to withdraw from the disorderly (1 Cor. 5:1-13; 2 Thess. 3:6-15).

The Meaning of Discipline

Discipline is not limited to "withdrawing." Just as the word "teaching" is not limited to oral instruction, discipline (while including withdrawing) includes much, much more.

The English word "discipline" defined. The American Heritage Dictionary defines the noun form as:[1]

---

1   https://ahdictionary.com/word/search.html?q=discipline.

1. Training expected to produce a specific character or pattern of behavior, especially training that produces moral or mental improvement: *was raised in the strictest discipline.*

2.
   a. Control obtained by enforcing compliance or order: *military discipline.*
   b. Controlled behavior resulting from disciplinary training; self-control: *Dieting takes a lot of discipline.*
   c. A state of order based on submission to rules and authority: *a teacher who demanded discipline in the classroom.*

3. Punishment intended to correct or train: *subjected to harsh discipline.*

4. A set of rules or methods, as those regulating the practice of a church or monastic order.

5. A branch of knowledge or teaching: *the discipline of mathematics.*

The verb form is defined as:

1. To train by instruction and practice, as in following rules or developing self-control: *The sergeant disciplined the recruits to become soldiers.* See Synonyms at teach.

2. To punish in order to gain control or enforce obedience. See Synonyms at punish.

3. To impose order on: *needed to discipline their study habits.*

Summarized, discipline includes training, instruction, teaching, punishment, and rules.

The word "discipline" as used in the Old Testament and New Testament. As we look at the use of our word in the Old and New Testaments, we must conclude that discipline includes instruction, warning, restraint, and correction.

Old Testament. We will only notice three examples from the book of Proverbs.

1. Proverbs 3:11-12 -
   "My son, do not despise the chastening of the Lord,
   nor detest His correction;
   For whom the Lord loves He corrects,
   just as a father the son *in whom* he delights."
The word "chastening" is translated "discipline" in the ESV, NIV, and NASB.[2] The same word is translated "instruction" several times in Proverbs (1:2, 3, 7, 8; 4:1, 13). In this text, discipline has the purpose of correction.

2. Proverbs 13:24 –
   "He who spares his rod hates his son,
   But he who loves him disciplines him promptly."
Strong's (Hebrew # 4148) defines the word "discipline" as "prop. *chastisement*; fig. *reproof, warning or instruction*; also, *restraint*."[3]

3. Proverbs 23:13 –
   "Do not withhold correction from a child,
   For *if* you beat him with a rod, he will not die."
The word "correction" is translated "discipline" in the ESV, NASB, and NIV. It is the same word translated "instruction" in verse 12.

New Testament. Here we see two examples that involve two different words.

1. 2 Timothy 3:16-17 – "All Scripture *is* given by inspiration of God, and *is* profitable for doctrine, for reproof, for correction, for instruction in righteousness, that the man of God may be complete, thoroughly equipped for every good work." The Scriptures were given for "instruction" (v. 17). The NKJV footnote says "discipline." The same word (translated "instruction" here) is translated "training" in Ephesians 6:4. It is translated "chastening" in Hebrews 12:5, 7, 8, 11.

---

2 The footnote to the NASB has "instruction."
3 Strong, J. (2009). *A Concise Dictionary of the Words in the Greek Testament and Th Hebrew Bible* (Vol. 2, p. 63). Bellingham, WA: Logos Bible Software.

The word is *paideia* which Thayer defines as,

> "1. *the whole training and education of children (which relates to the cultivation of mind and morals, and employs for this purpose now commands and admonitions, now reproof and punishment): Eph. 6:4 [cf. W. 388 (363) note]; (in Grk. writ. fr. Aeschyl. on, it includes also the care and training of the body.) [See esp. Trench, Syn. § xxxii.; cf. Jowett's Plato, index s. v. Education]. 2. whatever in adults also cultivates the soul, esp. by correcting mistakes and curbing the passions; hence a. instruction which aims at the increase of virtue: 2 Tim. 3:16.*"[4]

2. 1 Corinthians 9:27 – "But I discipline my body and bring *it* into subjection, lest, when I have preached to others, I myself should become disqualified."

This is self-discipline. The word translated "discipline" literally means to beat black and blue.[5] The idea seems to be that of beating a slave into subjection. The following translations may help us understand. The MEV says, "bring and keep my body under subjection." The NRSV, "punish my body and enslave it." The NET, "I subdue my body and make it a slave." The NCV, "I treat my body hard and make it a slave." The LBP (though not a good translation, but a good paraphrase) is helpful, "Like an athlete I punish my body, treating it roughly, training it to do what it should, not what it wants to do."

Much of what we do in the service of God is discipline. From all of the above, we learn that what we do in teaching (in classes and sermons), studying, worship and encouragement is part of church discipline.

Two Kinds of Discipline

Instructive – teaching. One form of discipline is instructive. Teaching the word of God can bring order to our lives. Moses said that God's commandments, statutes, and judgments (His revelation) had been given to "teach you, that you may observe *them*" (Deut. 6:1-4). Jesus said that those who come to God have "heard and learned from the Father" (John 6:44-45). The grace of God teaches us how to live (Titus 2:11-12). The inspired text is profitable for doctrine, reproof, correction and instruction (2 Tim. 3:16-17). Elders admonish the flock (1 Thess. 5:12).

---

[4] Thayer, J. H. (1889). *A Greek-English Lexicon of the New Testament: being Grimm's Wilke's Clavis Novi Testamenti* (p. 473). New York: Harper & Brothers.
[5] Thayer, *ibid.*, (p. 646).

As fellow Christians, we are to exhort one another (Heb. 3:12-13) and provoke one another unto love and good works (Heb. 10:24).

This form of discipline is preventative in nature. Alexander Campbell said, "To cut off an offender is good; to cure him is better, but to prevent him falling, is best of all."[6]

Corrective. Corrective discipline is necessary in the home (Prov. 22:15; Eph. 6:1-4; Heb. 12:5-12). In society, the lawless are to be punished (Rom. 13:1-7). When one sins against another, a personal rebuke is designed to produce a correction (Matt. 18:15-17). The unruly are to be warned (1 Thess. 5:14). The erring is to be identified (Rom. 16:17). Included in this is withdrawing from the disorderly (1 Cor. 5; 2 Thess. 3).

Corrective discipline (which will be a major portion of our study in this work) is only a part of the broader picture of church discipline.

The Means of Discipline[7]

Public Instruction. Paul taught in the public assembly at Troas (Acts 20:6-7). He also told the elders at Ephesus that he had taught them publicly as well as from house to house (Acts 20:20). Many sins are done in ignorance. Public instruction informs and leads the sinner to the right path. Many have corrected their ways because of what they learn from public instruction.

Private Instruction and Exhortation. Paul taught from house to house at Ephesus (Acts 20:20). The spiritual should seek to restore the erring (Gal. 6:1). Men, women and young people can be involved in this (cf. 2 Tim. 2:2).[8] Individual teaching can meet specific needs.

Private Rebuke and Admonition. Personal offenses should be handled privately (Matt. 18:15-17; Luke 17:3). This is an effort to keep a private matter a private matter. If this form of discipline is handled correctly, others may never know about it. If two people in a congregation are at odds and the

---

6   Alexander Campbell, *The Christian System*, 92.
7   The points here are taken from a tract by Cecil Willis on *Church Discipline*, 6-9.
8   The term "men" is from a word that means mankind which could include women.

pattern is followed as revealed in Matthew 18:15-17, others in the church may never know there was a problem.

Public Censure. There is a time for public rebuke. Paul rebuked Peter in the presence of others (Gal. 2:11-14). When sin is well-established in an elder, he should be rebuked before all (1 Tim. 5:20). At times, names need to be mentioned of those who lead others astray (1 Tim. 1:18-20; 2 Tim. 2:17-18; Rom. 16:17).

Social Ostracism. Those who are marked are to be avoided (Rom. 16:17). We should turn away from those who live in such a way to make the times perilous (2 Tim. 3:1-5). Some are to be rejected (Titus 3:10). The false teacher is not to be received (2 John 9-11). When we withdraw from the disorderly, we are not to have company (socialize) with them (1 Cor. 5:9-13; 2 Thess. 3:6-15). As we shall see in later studies, this is not an act of self-righteousness, but an effort to bring the erring to repentance and keep the church pure.

God's Use of Discipline[9]

Since the beginning of time, God has used discipline. When man rebelled, God punished the evildoer.

Adam and Eve were driven from the garden (Gen. 1:26-28; 2:8, 15-17; 3:22-24).

The flood destroyed the wicked of Noah's day (Gen. 6:5-7; 7:21-23).

Sodom and Gomorrah were burned for their immorality (Gen. 19:24-29).

Israel was sentenced to wander in the wilderness for their lack of faith (Num. 14:28-35).

The Sabbath breaker was to be stoned (Num. 15:35).

Moses was kept from the promised land because of his disobedience (Num. 20:12).

---

9   The points in this section are taken from Thomas G. O'Neal, *Walking in Truth,* Vol. 17, No. 3 (July – August – September, 1993).

Achan was stoned for taking of the forbidden spoil (Josh. 7:21-26).

The young prophet disobeyed and was killed (1 Kings 13).

Ananias and Sapphira were stuck dead because they lied (Acts 5:1-11).

Peter was publicly rebuked for his hypocrisy (Gal. 2:11-14).

Alexander and Hymenaeus were delivered unto Satan (1 Tim. 1:18-20).

The point of this lesson is to see what discipline is and that it involves far more than the act of withdrawing. While much of this work will focus on withdrawing, discipline is a much broader subject.

Questions

1. Why is discipline such an emotional issue? How should the faithful Christian address such emotional questions? _____
   _____
   _____
   _____

2. Why is discipline necessary? _____
   _____
   _____
   _____

3. What three principles are present in all areas where discipline is needed (home, sports, work, military, etc.)? _____
   _____
   _____
   _____

4. How does self-discipline relate to church discipline? _____
   _____
   _____
   _____

5. What do we learn from the definition of the English word discipline?
   _____
   _____
   _____

6. How do the passages in Proverbs help our understanding of discipline?
   _____
   _____
   _____

7. What do we learn about discipline from 2 Timothy 3:16-17? _____
   _____
   _____
   _____

8. What do we learn about discipline from 1 Corinthians 9:27 and the various translations of it? _____
   _____
   _____
   _____

9. List five different means of discipline. _____
   _____
   _____
   _____

10. What are the two kinds of discipline? _____
    _____
    _____

Personal Offenses

Lesson 2

This work addresses two kinds of offenses. (1) A *personal offense* is committed when one person sins against another. As we strive to save the erring, the church, our families, and ourselves, personal offenses must be addressed. (2) A *public offense* involves a sin that is not personal (or merely against another). Public offenses will be addressed in lesson 3.

Jesus addressed personal offenses in Matthew 18:10-20. These verses are in a context that deals with relationships. Verses 1-5 address the question of who is the greatest. The point is that humility is required in our relationship with others. Verses 6-9 focus on the one who offends (by causing another to sin). The point concerns responsibility we bear in our relationship with others. Verses 10-14 deal with the lost sheep. The lesson learned is the value of just one of the souls we deal with in our relationships. Verses 15-20 are about going to the offender. Differences must be resolved to restore and maintain good relationships. Finally, verses 21-35 are about the unforgiving servant. The lesson is that we must be willing to forgive those that sin against us.

Our focus here is on personal offenses—when one has been done wrong. Do you ever feel that you have been done wrong? What do you do? Who should you tell? How do you feel about the offender? Who is to say how you should react? Who should you have with you when you approach them? Jesus answers these questions in our text.

The Wrong Attitude (vv. 10-14)

Do not despise (v. 10). Jesus said, "Take heed that you do not despise one of these little ones" (Matt. 18:10).

What does "despise" mean? Strong defines it as **"to think against, i.e. disesteem:—despise."**[1] A. T. Robertson comments, "Literally, 'think down on,' with the assumption of superiority."[2] Lenski observes, "'to think down on' as though these little ones could be disregarded, as though they amounted to little or nothing."[3] To despise means to have contempt for another. John would call this attitude "hate" (i.e. lack of love – 1 John 3:15).

Why would one despise another? The context suggests the one despised has sinned. The verses just before verses 6-9 discuss one who is offended (another has caused them to sin). The verses immediately following compare those who are despised to sheep gone astray (vv. 12-14). The next section (vv. 15-17) addresses what to do if a brother sins against you. Then the last section of the chapter is about forgiveness of sin (vv. 21-35).

Could I be guilty? Like the disciples who asked, "Lord, is it I" (Matt. 26:22), we must ask if we could be guilty of despising a brother in Christ. Anytime I have bitter feelings, think someone is not worth my efforts, or view another as a "less" disciple, I am despising another.

Reasons we should not despise another. There are three reasons Jesus gave in the context for not despising:

Angels (v. 10). There is no evidence of personal "guardian angels" as some commentators have interpreted this passage. However, it may suggest that angels in some general way guard disciples. Angels work for us in some way (Heb. 1:14). Barnes observed, "He does not mean, I suppose, to state that every good man has his guardian angel, as many of the Jews believed; but that the angels were, in general, the guards of his followers, and aided them and watched over them."[4] If angels are concerned about them, how could I despise them?

---

1   Strong, J. (2009). *A Concise Dictionary of the Words in the Greek Testament and The Hebrew Bible* (Vol. 1, p. 41). Bellingham, WA: Logos Bible Software.
2   Robertson, A. T. (1933). *Word Pictures in the New Testament* (Mt 18:10). Nashville, TN: Broadman Press.
3   Lenski, R. C. H. (1961). *The Interpretation of St. Matthew's Gospel* (p. 691). Minneapolis, MN: Augsburg Publishing House.
4   Barnes, A. (1884–1885). *Notes on the New Testament: Matthew & Mark.* (R. Frew, Ed.) (p. 186). London: Blackie & Son.

Christ came to save them (v. 11). Since Christ came to save those that sin, how can I despise them?

The value of one soul (vv. 12-14). Jesus compares the one who sins to a sheep that goes astray and is worthy of leaving the ninety-nine to seek the lost. Every individual is still the object of God's love.

The Right Action (vv. 15-17)

Here we see a contrast to the previous section. Rather than despise (vv. 10-14), we should approach the offender with compassion (vv. 15-17).

The sin. The sin under consideration in this passage is a private sin (between two individuals and God), not a public matter. Jesus said, "if your brother sins *against you*" (v. 15, emphasis mine DVR). The private interview ("go and tell him his fault between you and him alone") tells us that the sin is private. Later, at the end of this discussion, Peter asks about a sin "against me" (v. 21).

The point. There are times that sin is a personal or private matter—something that is between the two individuals and God and should be handled that way. The lessons to learn are: (1) The more private matters are kept private, the less public trouble we will have. (2) Public matters are not to be treated as private matters. Often when someone addresses a teacher of error publicly, someone else is quick to say we should have gone to him privately first, making an appeal to this passage. However, this doesn't fit the situation of Matthew 18:15-17. When Peter publicly sinned, Paul rebuked him in the presence of all, rather than following the procedure of our text (Gal. 2:11-21).

The rebuke. There are three approaches that are laid out by our Lord.

Primary approach (1st step, v. 15). The offended is to go to the offender. Often the attitude of the offended is to say, "I'm not the one who did the wrong. He should come crawling to me!" To the contrary, Jesus said go to the offender. The offended is to inform the offender of his sin. This is a definite violation of the law, not mere hurt feelings. He goes with proof, not mere questions of whether he has done wrong. The purpose of this visit is to gain his brother and settle the matter. This is an attempt to keep a private matter private.

Albert Barnes commented on this verse,

> This is required to be done alone: 1st. That he may have an opportunity of explaining his conduct. In nine cases out of ten, where one supposes that he has been injured, a little friendly conversation would set the matter right and prevent difficulty. 2d. That he may have an opportunity of acknowledging his offence or making reparation, if he has done wrong. Many would be glad of such an opportunity, and it is our duty to furnish it by calling on them. 3d. That we may admonish them of their error if they have done an injury to the cause of religion. This should not be blazoned abroad. It can do no good—it does injury; it is what the enemies of religion wish. Christ is often wounded in the house of his friends; and religion, as well as an injured brother, often suffers by spreading such faults before the world.[5]

Secondary approach (2nd step, v. 16). The offended takes others with him (one or two more). These will serve as witnesses to establish what is said and done. But, they also appeal to the offender for Jesus spoke of the offender's refusal to "hear them" (v. 17). Surely, this would cause the offender to think about how serious the matter is.

What qualifications, if any, should one look for when selecting who to take as witnesses? There are none given in this text. However, other passages would help us in choosing those who would best serve the purpose. Those who are spiritually minded (Gal. 6:1) are best equipped to help restore the sinner. In an entirely different matter, Paul suggested that a difference could be settled by seeking the help of those who have some wisdom (1 Cor. 6:5). The offended who wants to do right would select a fair minded, level headed brother or sister who would even correct him should the witness see fault in him.

What does it take to settle the matter? In some cases, what was perceived to be a sin may not be a sin at all. In such a case, a simple explanation may settle the matter. In other cases, where sin is established, resolution requires repentance. In some cases, restitution may be required.

---

5 Barnes, A. (1884–1885). *Notes on the New Testament: Matthew & Mark*. (R. Frew, Ed.) (p. 187). London: Blackie & Son.

"Final" approach (3rd step, v. 17). If the offender has not made a change with the first two approaches, the offended is to now tell it to the church. It is now time to take this to the elders of the church for they have the oversight (Acts 20:28). More appeals will be made before any discussion of withdrawal. Again, the offender is made to consider the seriousness of the matter.

If he does not hear (by responding with repentance), then "let him be to you like a heathen and a tax collector" (v. 17). This expression seems to be parallel to delivering him to Satan (1 Cor. 5:5), purging out the old leaven (1 Cor. 5:7), putting away the evil person (1 Cor. 5:13), withdrawing from the disorderly (2 Thess. 3:6), and noting that person (2 Thess. 3:15).

The purpose (the value of the limited approach).[6] (1) *It makes it easier to settle the problem.* The more people involved, the harder it is to settle. There is a danger of partiality and factionalism. We should always strive toward the goal of unity (Eph. 4:3).

(2) *It limits the impact on weaker brethren.* We must watch for how our actions affect those who are weaker (1 Thess. 5:14). If every private matter became a public discussion and tried in a public way, the church would be in a constant uproar.

(3) *It keeps the church from being distracted from its primary work of reaching the lost.* The work of the church is to spread the gospel (1 Tim. 3:15). "When a matter of private offense is broached to the overseers of the church it is not their duty or privilege to inquire into the matter immediately. Rather, it is their obligation to inquire if the scriptural procedure has been followed by the aggrieved party."[7]

(4) *Keeps the world from blaspheming the gospel of Christ.* Our conduct can cause the gospel of Christ to be blasphemed (Tit. 2:5; 1 Tim. 5:13-14). It does harm to the cause of Christ to parade our personal differences before the world.

---

6   The four points presented here are taken from W. Carl Ketcherside, *A Clean Church*, 24-27. This book was written long before he became ultra-liberal advancing the unity in diversity concept. In his later years he no longer accepted the principles taught in his own book.
7   Ketcherside, *ibid.*, 26.

The Authority that Works (vv. 18-20)

It might appear that our Lord shifted to a new subject in this section. However, this well connects with the previous verses (vv. 15-17).

Approved by God (v. 18). What we do in discipline should be approved by God. How one handles personal offenses must first be approved by God. What we do as a congregation must first be approved by God. What starts as a personal sin, may, in the end, bind action on all the rest.

Appeal to God (vv. 19-20). Jesus said that if two agree and ask of the Father, He will hear them. In the prayer of two (i.e. the offended and offender, v. 15), Christ is there, and it is effective. God hears the prayer of the offended, offender, and the witnesses (v. 16) as well. All need not be involved to make it work. If there is a problem between two and they settle it and pray, no one else need be there (i.e. the elders or preacher).

When a Christian wrongs you, do not despise them. Go to them with compassion. Settle the difference. Then, forgive.

Questions

1. What is a personal offense? _____
   _____
   _____

2. What does it mean to despise another Christian? _____
   _____
   _____

3. In the context of Matthew 18, why would one possibly despise another?
   _____
   _____
   _____

4. What reasons are given for not despising another? _____
   _____
   _____
   _____

5. What type of sin is under consideration in verses 15-17, and how do you know? _____

6. What is the primary approach (v. 15)? _____

7. What is the secondary approach (v. 16)? _____

8. What is the final approach (v. 17)? _____

9. What qualifications, if any, should be considered in selecting the witnesses to speak with the offender (v. 16)? _____

10. How does the discussion of authority (vv. 18-20) relate to the discussion of verses 15-17? _____

Public Offenses

Lesson 3

As we strive to save the erring, the church, our families, and ourselves, we must address public offenses. Public offenses (in contrast to personal offenses) are not merely between two Christians. These might include forsaking the assembly, drinking, adultery, bad language, and false teaching.

Public is not Private

Examples of public offenses. There are several instances of public offenses throughout the New Testament. The case of fornication at Corinth was known (1 Cor. 5). Those who were lazy and busybodies were known to the whole church (2 Thess. 3). The hypocrisy of Peter and Barnabas was before others (Gal. 2:11-21). The disruption of public worship in the cases of the abuse of the Lord's Supper (1 Cor. 11) and the misuse of tongues (1 Cor. 14) would obviously be public offenses. The arrogant mistreatment of others with the thinking that speaking in tongues was the superior gift (1 Cor. 4:6; 12-13) is another example. The false teaching concerning the resurrection (1 Cor. 15:12) was public. The private matter between Euodia and Syntyche had reached a point that Paul addressed it in a public way (Phil. 4:2).

The rules of Matthew 18:15-17 do not apply. This passage is misapplied when used in public matters. When some brother teaches error and a public response is made, someone is sure to say, "You should have gone to him first," and then they cite the Matthew text. Or, someone may suggest that this should have been settled privately. The same contention is made when some Christian sins publicly. Someone may say, "That was settled privately." When the elders go and talk with him, someone may contend that each one should have gone personally as Matthew 18 teaches.

Matthew 18:15-17 deals with a personal offense between two parties and should not to be applied to public matters.[1]

Public offenses are not to be settled privately. There is a principle set forth by Paul when he and Silas were in jail and officers were sent to tell them they could go. Paul's response was, "They have beaten us openly, uncondemned Romans, and have thrown us into prison. And now do they put us out secretly? No indeed! Let them come themselves and get us out" (Acts 16:37). While this is not totally parallel, the principle to be learned is that when an offense is public, you do not settle it privately.

Can you imagine the situation of the fornicator at Corinth (1 Cor. 5; 2 Cor. 2) being settled privately? Can you imagine Peter's hypocrisy being resolved privately (Gal. 2:11-21)?

Paul addressed the problems at Corinth (fornication, lack of discipline, going to law with a brother, abuse of the Lord's Supper, confusion over spiritual gifts, and false teaching) publicly with the whole church in the first Corinthian letter.

Seeking to Restore the Erring

Paul wrote, "Brethren, if a man is overtaken in any trespass, you who are spiritual restore such a one in a spirit of gentleness, considering yourself lest you also be tempted" (Gal. 6:1). When one is erring, we should seek to restore him *before* giving any consideration to withdrawing.[2]

The one who needs to be restored. The erring is involved in the practice of sin and thus stands in need. Our text (Gal. 6:1) says he was overtaken in a trespass ("transgression" ESV, "sin" NET). The word "overtaken" suggests an element of surprise. "The verb means lit. *to take before; to anticipate or forestall.* Elsewhere only Mk. 14:8; 1 Cor. 11:21. LXX, Wisd. 18:17. Not, *be*

---

[1] Go back to lesson 2 for evidence that this passage deals with personal offenses.
[2] As an elder and preacher, I have been to visit with many who are erring. On the first visit or two if anything is said about withdrawing, they bring it up, not me. When they do, I tell them that is not on our mind at the present. We are trying to *restore* them before we reach that point.

detected in the act by some one else *before he can escape*, but *surprised by the fault itself,* hurried into error."[3]

James describes the erring as one who "wanders from the truth," "a sinner," in "error," and guilty of a "multitude of sins" (James 5:19-20).

We must make sure the charge is correct when seeking to restore the erring. An unfounded accusation can be damaging. Paul cited his reliable source when addressing problems at Corinth (1 Cor. 1:11; 5:1-2). The witnesses that one takes with him in the secondary approach (Matt. 18:16) provide evidence. A charge against an elder is to be established by two or three witnesses (1 Tim. 5:19).

The one who seeks to help. All Christians have some responsibility in trying to restore the erring (Gal. 6:1; James 5:19-20; 1 Thess. 5:14). It is not merely the work of elders and preachers.

Those who are *spiritual* are charged with the responsibility (Gal. 6:1). The context immediately preceding this text describes the spiritual man as one who is led and governed by the Spirit's teaching (Gal. 5:16-26). Notice the parallel expressions: "Walk in the Spirit" (v. 16), "led by the Spirit" (v. 18), "fruit of the Spirit" (v. 22), "live in the Spirit" (v. 25), and "walk in the Spirit" (v. 25).

Those correcting others, being spiritual, will not be guilty of the same kind of sin. To approach another about their sin when guilty of the same renders the efforts ineffective (Matt. 7:1-5; Rom. 2:21-23).

What needs to be done. Our text says we are to seek to restore the erring (Gal. 6:1). The word for "restore" is the same word translated "mending the nets" (Matt. 4:21). It is also the same word Paul used when he urged his readers to "perfect" what was lacking (1 Thess. 3:10). The word means, "*to strengthen, perfect, complete, make one what he ought to be*...Gal. 6:1 (of one who by correction may be brought back into the right way)."[4]

---

3   Vincent, M. R. (1887). *Word Studies in the New Testament* (Vol. 4, pp. 170–171). New York: Charles Scribner's Sons.
4   Thayer, J. H. (1889). *A Greek-English Lexicon of the New Testament* (p. 336). New York: Harper & Brothers.

All that we do should be done in a manner to bring about the goal of restoring the lost, always avoiding anything that is detrimental to it.

How is it to be done? The erring need to be *warned*. Paul said that we should warn the unruly[5] (1 Thess. 5:14). The danger of dying in an erring condition demands a warning be given (John 8:21). When the church gets involved in trying to reach the erring, the brethren should be urging the person to change before giving any thought to withdrawing.

The spiritual person will *exhort and encourage* the erring to be led by the Spirit's instructions (consider the context of Gal. 6), as he is led.

There will be times that a *public rebuke* is needed. Paul rebuked Peter "before *them* all" (Gal. 2:14). Elders that sin should be rebuked "in the presence of all" (1 Tim. 5:20).

The attitude needed when seeking to restore others. Our text (Gal. 6) first describes the proper attitude one should have *toward the erring*. The approach should be with the "spirit of gentleness." The same word for "gentleness" is translated "meekness" (James 1:21), and "humility" (Titus 3:2). We must approach the erring with a humble and calm spirit.

> With a kind, forbearing, and forgiving spirit; Note, Mat. 5:5. Not with anger; not with a lordly and overbearing mind; not with a love of finding others in fault, and with a desire for inflicting the discipline of the church; not with a harsh and unforgiving temper, but with love, and gentleness, and humility, and patience, and with a readiness to forgive when wrong has been done. This is an essential qualification for restoring and recovering an offending brother.[6]

Secondly, the attitude *toward self* should be that the one considers himself (Gal. 6:1). Considering self is part of the humility of gentleness. The NCV translates this, "But be careful, because you might be tempted to sin, too." The point is, do not act as if you would never stumble. Always approach him as you would want him to approach you.

---

5 The word "unruly" is from the same word translated "disorderly" (2 Thess. 3:6).
6 Albert Barnes. (1884-1885), *Notes on the New Testament: II Corinthians & Galatians.* (R. Frew, Ed.) (p. 391). London: Blackie & Son.

Dealing with Teachers of Error

What do we do when false teachers arise among brethren? What if a false teacher arises within the local church? What if a man we support starts teaching error? What if we learn that a man we have scheduled for a meeting is teaching error? If a very influential brother starts teaching error, should the local church be warned? In some of the situations raised here, a local church would not withdraw from someone, but certainly would not extend fellowship.

Identified. Paul says that those who cause divisions and offenses contrary to the doctrine should be *noted* (Rom. 16:17). The KJV uses the word, "mark." It is the same word used for noting good examples to follow (Phil. 3:17). It means "Keep an eye on so as to avoid."[7] Lenski observed, "The rendering, 'mark them who' (A. V.) in our versions implies that such errorists were present in Rome; they were not, but some of them might drift into Rome at any time, and 'look out for them' sounds the warning to be on guard."[8]

There are times when it is necessary to identify a false teacher by name. Paul mentions Hymenaeus and Alexander by name (1 Tim. 1:18-20). Later he identifies Hymenaeus and Philetus (2 Tim. 2:16-18). John calls Diotrephes by name (3 John 8-10).

Avoided. Having noted those who cause divisions, Paul says "avoid them" (Rom. 16:17). Vincent says that means to "*turn aside.*"[9] The ASV renders this, "turn away from them." This is not a suggestion to avoid their doctrine but to avoid associating with them. Rather the text says "avoid them." Lenski makes this point: "Mark the aorist imperative ἐκκλίνατε and note the force of ἐκ plus ἀπό: 'definitely, decisively, once for all, incline away from them'—'from them,' not merely from their teaching, 'from them' because of their teaching. 'Avoid them' (A. V.) is the sense: have nothing to do with them. 'Turn away from them' (R. V.) with finality."[10]

---

[7] Robertson, A. T. (1933). *Word Pictures in the New Testament* (Ro 16:17). Nashville, TN: Broadman Press.

[8] Lenski, R. C. H. (1936). *The Interpretation of St. Paul's Epistle to the Romans* (p. 915). Columbus, Ohio: Lutheran Book Concern.

[9] Vincent, M. R. (1887). *Word Studies in the New Testament* (Vol. 3, pp. 181). New York: Charles Scribner's Sons.

[10] Lenski, R. C. H. (1936). *The Interpretation of St. Paul's Epistle to the Romans* (p. 916). Columbus, Ohio: Lutheran Book Concern.

Paul tells Titus, "Reject a divisive man after the first and second admonition" (Titus 3:10). The ESV renders this "have nothing more to do with him." The NIV says, "have nothing to do with them."

Reasons for identifying and avoiding false teachers. (1) We are not to fellowship false teachers (2 John 9-11). (2) False teachers, even among brethren, are enemies of the cross (Phil. 3:18). (3) They lead others to commit sin (2 Tim. 2:16-18; 1 Cor. 15:33).

Elders have a responsibility to warn the flock about dangers—including false teachers among brethren.

Questions

1. Define public offense. _____
   _____
   _____

2. List a few examples from the New Testament of public offenses. ____
   _____
   _____
   _____

3. Why should a public matter not be settled privately? _____
   _____
   _____
   _____

4. In what sense does "overtaken" (Gal. 6:1) suggest an element of surprise? _____
   _____
   _____

5. Who is a spiritual person (Gal. 6:1)? _____
   _____
   _____
   _____

6. How is the work of restoring the erring to be done? _____
   _____
   _____
   _____

7. Why would a public rebuke ever be needed? _____
   _____
   _____

8. What attitude should we have toward the erring? _____
   _____
   _____

9. What should be our attitude toward ourselves as we approach the erring? _____
   _____
   _____
   _____

10. What reasons can be given for a local church dealing publicly with false teachers? _____
    _____
    _____

The Forgotten and Misunderstood Command

Lesson 4

It is a command to withdraw from those who persist in sin (2 Thess. 3:6; 1 Cor. 5:1-13). Yet, it is a command that has been forgotten and greatly misunderstood. The difficulty is not because the text is unclear, but because of human involvement with emotions that pull at the heart.

The Forgotten Command

It had been forgotten at Corinth. The sin of fornication was well established (1 Cor. 5:1). The brethren were not bothered or concerned enough to take proper action (1 Cor. 5:2). The church had been instructed sometime before that such inaction was wrong (1 Cor. 5:9). They seem to have forgotten the command.

It is forgotten in many churches today. Churches forget this command in different ways. In some cases, it is mere neglect (cf. Heb. 2:3; Neh. 8:13-18). In some cases, it is willful ignoring (Rom. 10:3, 17).

Some churches forget to teach on the subject. Whether it is because they view the subject as of little importance or they think it will not be practiced anyway, some places have little or no teaching on it.

Some churches forget to practice it. With some, withdrawing is not practiced at all. With others, it is practiced only in "extreme" cases (i.e. fornication). Some are inconsistent in their practice. When it is not practiced, churches create an environment where members (like undisciplined children) realize how far they can go without any discipline. Someone can miss a lot of services and nothing is said or done. One can participate in worldliness, and no action is taken. There can be a case of divorce and remarriage, and no questions are asked.

It is not only withdrawal that is forgotten. In some places, even preventative discipline, teaching, etc, is missing. When one is involved in doing wrong, the rebuke and correction (that should precede any withdrawal) are missing at times.

Why is it forgotten? Several reasons can be suggested.

1. *In some places, it is not taught.* Thus, we have a generation arise that does not know what the Bible says on the subject (cf. Jud. 2:10).

2. *Some have never seen the withdrawal process at work.*

3. *Others use human wisdom, thinking they know a better way of reaching the erring* (cf. Rom. 11:34).

4. *It is the easier course.* Because it is unpleasant, it is easier not to withdraw than to press on and do what God demands.

5. *Some have seen it abused.* It is possible to withdraw with the wrong motive (i.e. revenge). Likewise, it is possible to be disciplined when there is no evidence of wrong. Some who have witnessed such abuse are ready to throw discipline out altogether. Although some have abused the Lord's Supper, baptism, and the gospel, we do not see fit to forget them.

6. *Many are afraid.* Fear of hurting the feelings of the one in sin or his family may cause some to be reluctant. It may sever relationships or even drive people away, so some churches will not practice it. The possibility of losing members, losing the money they contribute, and even facing a lawsuit make some scared to proceed.

The Misunderstood Command

Some brethren misunderstand what it is, how it is practiced, and what it means. Misunderstanding any question or issue hinders a proper understanding by creating a barrier. Let's illustrate: The Jews had the misconception that the Messiah would remain forever and not die (John 12:34). That misunderstanding kept them from seeing that Jesus, who said He would die, was the Messiah (John 12:32-33). Likewise, one who thinks the teaching that baptism is essential means one is saved by water will never see that baptism is essential (Mark 16:16). That misunderstanding creates a barrier to grasping the truth. Again, if one thinks there are no miracles today, then one concludes God is not working at all and their understanding that miracles have ceased is hampered (1 Cor. 13:8-10).

The misunderstandings listed below (and others) create a similar barrier to one seeing the truth revealed in 1 Corinthians 5 and 2 Thessalonians 3.

"Withdrawing is kicking them out of the church." No one is being kicked out of the church. We cannot do that. God adds (Acts 2:47). Thus, God removes. What we are doing is withdrawing ourselves from the unfaithful. We are to put away the wicked person (1 Cor. 5:13). We are to withdraw ourselves (2 Thess. 3:6). No fellowship can be maintained with darkness (Eph. 5:11).

Rather than an effort to kick one out, it is an effort to bring him back (1 Cor. 5:5). Church discipline is like the chastening of children. We do not apply correction to children to teach them to be unloving, but rather to teach love, obedience, and reverence (Heb. 12:9-11).

"Withdrawal is a prohibition to attend." No one has ever been asked not to attend.[1] In fact, just the opposite is the case. Faithful brethren would encourage those who have been disciplined to continue to attend. Hopefully, by the classes they attend and the sermons they hear, they will have a change of heart. Hopefully, by the influence and encouragement of other Christians, they will turn back to the Lord.

"Withdrawing doesn't do any good." This is based on the idea that those who are erring are not brought back by withdrawal. In fact, some think it will likely push them away.

It brought the fornicator at Corinth to repentance. The church was told to withdraw (1 Cor. 5:1-13). They did, and he repented (2 Cor. 2:3-11). We have seen it work (bringing the erring back) in modern times as well.

Admittedly, it does not always cause the sinner to return. That does not mean it does not work. Church discipline is like spanking children (Prov.

---

1 There may be extreme cases where a person has been disruptive in the assembly or made threats and thus the elders ask them not to attend.

22:15). When it does not work, it may be that we have been inconsistent or did not administer it firmly and timely.

While the wayward may not always return, there is yet another purpose (keeping the church pure – 1 Cor. 5:6-7) that is always accomplished!

"Withdrawing cannot be done in love." At times, we are told, "Instead of withdrawing, we should LOVE them!" This misconception assumes love and discipline cannot be harmonized. That is like assuming one cannot harmonize salvation by blood and by baptism. It is also like assuming one cannot harmonize love and spanking a child (Prov. 13:24).

When there is such a misunderstanding of love, one cannot see what the text says. When one holds to the idea that love means a parent will not spank, he will not see what the text says about using the rod (Prov. 22:15). Likewise, when one holds to the idea that love means that we will not withdraw or withhold association, he will not be able to see what the text says about withdrawing and having no company with the disciplined (1 Cor. 5; 2 Thess. 3).

Love for God and the lost souls means that we will follow God's plan for saving the erring (1 Cor. 5:5).

"We can't be friendly and kind to those from whom we withdraw." Some have the idea that we cannot show kindness to those from whom we withdraw. The idea is that if we see them in public we ought to avoid them, or we cannot stop and ask how they are doing. This misconception equates kindness and friendliness with approving of their life.

The restrictions found in the withdrawing passages involve putting the evil person away (1 Cor. 5:13; 2 Thess. 3:6). Also, the faithful are not to "company" with them (1 Cor. 5:11; 2 Thess. 3:14). Neither of those restrictions forbids speaking and being kind.

Let us not forget that we are not to treat the disciplined one as an enemy, but continue to admonish him as a brother (2 Thess. 3:15). That hardly can be done if we cannot even be kind enough to speak to our brother.

"Withdrawing is giving up on the person." When we withdraw, we are not giving up, but merely making an additional effort to save him (1 Cor. 5:5-6). We are hardly giving up if we are continuing to admonish him as a brother (2 Thess. 3:15). Even though we are not giving up, there comes a time that we let him be as a heathen and a tax collector (Matt. 18:17). There comes a time that we deliver him to Satan as we put him away from among us (1 Cor. 5:5).

These are just a few of the misunderstandings of the subject. In other lessons in this study, we will address additional questions and arguments against it.

Questions

1. Should the church at Corinth have already known their responsibility to the fornicator before receiving the first Corinthian letter? _____
   _____
   _____

2. What are two ways we can forget the commands of God? _____
   _____
   _____

3. When church discipline is not practiced as it should be, what kind of environment is created in the local church? _____
   _____
   _____

4. In what way has withdrawal been abused, causing some to forget the command? _____
   _____
   _____

5. What makes some afraid to practice withdrawing? _____
   _____
   _____

6. How does one's misunderstanding on some issue prevent them from seeing the truth? _____
_____
_____

7. How would you respond to the misunderstanding that claims withdrawal is kicking people out of the church? _____
_____
_____

8. How would you respond to the misunderstanding that says it does not do any good? _____
_____
_____

9. How would you respond to the misunderstanding that says it cannot be done in love? _____
_____
_____

10. Does withdrawal mean we cannot be kind and friendly with those who have been disciplined? Explain your answer. _____
_____
_____
_____

The Purpose of Withdrawing and From Whom Should We Withdraw?

Lesson 5

It is imperative that we understand (1) the purpose of withdrawing and (2) those from whom we should withdraw. When we see the purpose, we will see its importance. Much of the controversy and confusion over church discipline is due to not understanding these two principles.

The Purpose of Withdrawing

God has a purpose for everything He commands us to do. If withdrawing is a command (1 Cor. 5; 2 Thess. 3), then it has an important purpose. "The scriptures do suggest, however, that discipline has both a corrective and protective function."[1]

Corrective function – to save the erring. Withdrawing should only take place after repeated efforts have been made to restore the erring brother (Gal. 6:1; James 5:19-20).

The church at Corinth is told to put the fornicator away from them "that his spirit may be saved in the day of the Lord Jesus" (1 Cor. 5:5). The Thessalonians are instructed to withdraw from the disorderly brother "that he may be ashamed" (2 Thess. 3:14). The purpuse is that he might be ashamed of his sinful conduct and repent. "The purpose of church discipline is always to bring the sinner to this repentant shame and thus to win him back."[2] Furthermore, they are to continue to "admonish" him (v. 15). Why admonish him? This is a continual effort to win him back.

---

1. Wayne Jackson, *Christian Courier*, Vol. XXVI, No. 9, January 1991.
2. Lenski, R. C. H. (1937). *The Interpretation of St. Paul's Epistles to the Colossians, to the Thessalonians, to Timothy, to Titus and to Philemon* (pp. 467–468). Columbus, OH: Lutheran Book Concern.

When Jesus gave direction for dealing with personal offenses (Matt. 18:15-17), all three approaches (including the church action) are for the purpose of gaining the brother. Paul says he delivered Hymenaeus and Alexander to Satan "that they may learn not to blaspheme" (1 Tim. 1:19-20).

Protective function–to save others. The impact upon others is two-fold.

1. *It is to keep the church pure.* God wants the church to be pure. He cleanses those who are added to the church (Eph. 5:26-27; 1 Pet. 1:22). We are told to live separate from the world (2 Cor. 6:14–7:1).

Discipline is designed to maintain the purity of the church. Paul rebukes the Corinthians for tolerating the fornicator asking, "Do you not know that a little leaven leavens the whole lump?" (1 Cor. 5:6). "The sense here is plain. A single sin indulged in, or allowed in the church, would act like leaven—it would pervade and corrupt the whole church, unless it was removed. On this ground, and for this reason, discipline should be administered, and the corrupt member should be removed."[3] Thus, they are instructed to "purge out the old leaven, that you may be a new lump" (v. 7). Because of this permeating influence, Paul instructs to "put away from yourselves the evil person" (v. 13).

2. *It causes others to learn and fear.* This principle is seen in the Old Testament when a rebellious son is brought to the elders of the city and the men of the city stone him with stones. Thus, "all Israel shall hear and fear" (Deut. 21:18-21).

Others within the church learn and fear when they see disciplinary action. When the brethren saw what happened to Ananias and Sapphira, "great fear came upon all the church" (Acts 5:11). When elders who sin are rebuked before all, "the rest also may fear" (1 Tim. 5:20).

The impact is upon people in the world as well. The case of Ananias and Sapphira caused fear to come upon the church "and upon all who heard these things" (Acts 5:11). People of the world take note when they hear the church has reprimanded a member by withdrawing from him. Several years ago this writer had a study going with a young lady who was raised in

---

3   Barnes, A. (1884–1885). *Notes on the New Testament: I Corinthians.* (R. Frew, Ed.) (p. 87). London: Blackie & Son.

the Baptist church. She had been attending our worship services for a few weeks. One Sunday morning when she was present, the elders announced that the church is withdrawing from five people. My first thought was that she would not understand why we called the names of these five in the assembly and identified their sin. I wondered if she would be offended thinking that this was the wrong way to handle people. To my surprise, she was very pleased and said, "I'm glad to find a church that deals with sin. We didn't do anything like this in the Baptist church!"

Without it, we have many problems. 1. The erring persisting in sin will be lost. The fornicator at Corinth would not have repented if the church had not withdrawn from him (1 Cor. 5; 2 Cor. 2). 2. The church will be corrupted (cf. 1 Cor. 5:6). 3. The influence of preaching will be lessened and neutralized because the teaching doesn't have any "teeth." 4. There will be a spiritual and moral decline (1 Cor. 5:6). 5. We will not be pleasing to God because we are not obeying His command (1 Cor. 5; 2 Thess. 3).

From Whom Should We Withdraw?

A word of caution is in order. It is important that we understand the difference between *a babe in Christ* and a *Christian who has had time to grow and mature.* Paul rebuked some who had plenty of time to grow but had not (Heb. 5:12-14). The same writer makes a distinction in one who is unruly, one who is weak, and one who is discouraged (1 Thess. 5:14).

There is a need for longsuffering and patience as we deal with others (Gal. 5:22; Col. 1:11; 3:12; Psa. 86:15). This does not mean that we ignore the sin. It simply means we exhaust every means of seeking to restore the erring before we withdraw from them.

General Rules. The church withdraws from one who is a erring Christian. The instructions given to Corinth concern a fornicator "among you" (v. 1). The leaven (the sinner and his sin) is within the lump (the church) (vv. 6-7). Paul clarifies that he is not talking about dealing with the sinner in the world (v. 10). The next verse clarifies that a church is dealing with a sinner who is a brother (1 Cor. 5:11). The brethren are to judge those who are "inside" (1 Cor. 5:12). Twice in the second Thessalonian letter, the writer clarifies that withdrawal is for one who claims to be a brother (cf. 3:6, 15).

The church disciplines one within the local church. Each local church is autonomous (Acts 20:28; 1 Pet. 5:1-3). The elders of one church have no oversight of another congregation. The fornicator was in the church (at Corinth) that was instructed to put him away (1 Cor. 5).[4]

Churches must be consistent when withdrawing from the disorderly. God does not show partiality and expects the same of His people (Rom. 2:11; 1 Tim. 5:21; Jas. 2:1-9; 3:17). We are to withdraw from "every brother" who walks disorderly (2 Thess. 3:6).

The disorderly. The one from whom we should withdraw is one who walks disorderly (2 Thess. 3:6). The word translated "disorderly" (ατακōs) is a military term meaning not keeping rank. W. E. Vine defines the word:

A. Adjective.
ataktos (ἄτακτος, 813) signifies "not keeping order" (a, negative, tasso, "to put in order, arrange"); it was especially a military term, denoting "not keeping rank, insubordinate"; it is used in 1 Thess. 5:14, describing certain church members who manifested an insubordinate spirit, whether by excitability or officiousness or idleness. See UNRULY.

B. Adverb.
ataktos (ἀτάκτως, 814) signifies "disorderly, with slackness" (like soldiers not keeping rank) 2 Thess. 3:6; in v. 11 it is said of those in the church who refused to work, and became busybodies (cf. 1 Tim. 5:13).

C. Verb.
atakteo (ἀτακτέω, 812) signifies "to be out of rank, out of one's place, undisciplined, to behave disorderly": in the military sense, "to break rank"; negatively in 2 Thess. 3:7, of the example set by the apostle and his fellow missionaries, in working for their bread while they were at Thessalonica so as not to burden the saints. See BEHAVE.[5]

---

[4] When a church withdraws from a brother, should other brethren (who are not members of that local congregation) honor or respect that action by not keeping company with him? That question will be addressed in lesson 13.

[5] Vine, W. E., Unger, M. F., & White, W., Jr. (1996). *Vine's Complete Expository Dictionary of Old and New Testament Words* (Vol. 2, p. 174). Nashville, TN: T. Nelson.

Thayer defines the word, "ἄ-τακτος, -ον, (τάσσω), *disorderly, out of the ranks*, (often so of soldiers)...*deviating from the prescribed order or rule*. 1 Th. 5:14, cf. 2 Th. 3:6." [6]

Albert Barnes observes, "A 'disorderly walk' denotes conduct that is in any way contrary to the rules of Christ. The proper idea of the word used here (ἀτάκτως), is that of soldiers who do not keep the ranks; who are regardless of order; and then who are irregular in any way. The word would include any violation of the rules of Christ on any subject."[7]

The same word is translated "unruly." "Now we exhort you, brethren, warn those who are *unruly*, comfort the fainthearted, uphold the weak, be patient with all" (1 Thess. 5:14, emphasis mine DVR). This text also mentions the fainthearted (discouraged) and the weak as being different than the unruly. Thus, we learn that the disorderly (unruly) are not the same as being fainthearted or weak.

The context of 2 Thessalonians 3:6 helps us to see how the word disorderly is used. First, he "walks" disorderly suggesting a continuance in the disorderly conduct (v. 6). His behavior is not according to the tradition of the apostles (v. 6). Neither is he obeying the word of the epistle (v. 14).

Specifically. The specifics given here are not exhaustive, for the term "disorderly" is broader than this list. The following passages mention some specific people in dealing with discipline.
- Fornicator (1 Cor. 5:1-2).
- Covetous (1 Cor. 5:11).
- Idolater (1 Cor. 5:11).
- Reviler (1 Cor. 5:11).
- Drunkard (1 Cor. 5:11).
- Extortioner (1 Cor. 5:11).
- Lazy (2 Thess. 3:11).
- Busybody (2 Thess. 3:11).
- One who sins against another and does not repent (Matt. 18:17).
- Teachers of error (Rom. 16:17-18; 1 Tim. 1:19-20).
- Factious (Tit. 3:10).

---

6   Thayer, J. H. (1889). *A Greek-English Lexicon of the New Testament: Being Grimm's Wilke's Clavis Novi Testamenti* (p. 83). New York: Harper & Brothers.

7   Barnes, A. (1884–1885). *Notes on the New Testament: I Thessalonians to Philemon*. (R. Frew, Ed.) (p. 99). London: Blackie & Son.

Knowing the two-fold purpose that God has for withdrawing and the ones from whom we should withdraw helps clear some of the confusion and controversy.

Questions

1. Discipline has both a _____ and a _____ function.

2. What should be done before we start thinking about withdrawing from the erring? _____

3. How does withdrawing from the erring help in saving his soul? _____

4. Cite an example from the Bible where withdrawing from someone caused him to repent. _____

5. How does withdrawing from the erring keep the church pure? _____

6. What impact does church discipline have upon the world around us? _____

7. What problems are created when a church does not practice withdrawing? _____

8. What general rules are given about those from whom we withdraw? _____

9. Define "disorderly." _____

10. What does 1 Thessalonians 5:14 teach us about one who is disorderly? _____

The Case at Corinth (Part 1)

Lesson 6

There are two notable cases of discipline in the New Testament: Corinth (1 Cor. 5) and Thessalonica (2 Thess. 3). Each of these provides an occasion for the Lord to reveal His teaching and for us to examine the instruction and learn.

This lesson focuses on the case at Corinth (1 Cor. 5) and the next two lessons focus on the case at Thessalonica.

The Problem (v. 1) – A Fornicator in Their Midst

Well reported. The KJV says "reported commonly," and the NKJV and ASV say "actually reported." The word translated "commonly" or "actually" (Strong's # 3654) means, "completely, i.e. altogether; (by anal.) everywhere; (neg.) not by any means:—at all, commonly, utterly."[1] A. T. Robertson observes, "Literally, wholly, altogether,...So papyri have it for 'really' and also for 'generally' or 'everywhere' as is possible here."[2] Thus, the report is generally known and accurate.

Fornication. This word refers to "illicit sexual intercourse."[3] "The word means, "sexual immorality, sexual sin of a general kind, that includes many different behaviors."[4] This term includes pre-marital relationships, extra-marital relationships, incest, and bestiality.

---

1 Strong, J. (2009). *A Concise Dictionary of the Words in the Greek Testament and The Hebrew Bible* (Vol. 1, p. 51). Bellingham, WA: Logos Bible Software.
2 Robertson, A. T. (1933). *Word Pictures in the New Testament* (1 Co 5:1). Nashville, TN: Broadman Press.
3 Vine, W. E., Unger, M. F., & White, W., Jr. (1996). *Vine's Complete Expository Dictionary of Old and New Testament Words* (Vol. 2, p. 252). Nashville, TN: T. Nelson.
4 Swanson, J. (1997). *Dictionary of Biblical Languages with Semantic Domains: Greek (New Testament)* (electronic ed.). Oak Harbor: Logos Research Systems, Inc.

Had his father's wife. The father may have still been living (2 Cor. 7:12).[5] The woman involved would not be the man's mother, but the father's second wife (perhaps a woman much younger than the father – closer to the son's age). Thus, the son and the step-mother developed a relationship. There is no evidence that the woman was a member of the church. Paul says nothing about dealing with her.

Not heard among the Gentiles. Paul says this is "such sexual immorality as is not even named among the Gentiles" (v. 1). It is not that it did not happen or exist among the Gentiles, but they did not tolerate it as the church at Corinth had done. "It would create the thought in the minds of the people of the world that the state or standard of morals was lower in the church than among the idolatrous heathen."[6]

The Failure (v. 2) – Not Dealt with the Fornicator Properly

Puffed up. This means they were filled with pride. Their pride was not because of the fornication or their toleration of it. Though, that could be possible in some circumstances. The person could be prominent, have money or be influential. Thus, they could be proud of the fact that such a person was in their midst in spite of their fornication. Or, a church could boast that they were tolerant and accepted those that other churches rejected. However, none of that seems to be the case here. They were filled with pride in spite of the actual condition of the church.

Why would they be filled with pride? Likely, it had to do with their view of spiritual gifts (1 Cor. 1:7; 4:6). Or, perhaps, there were other things they thought to be great about the church. Whatever the cause, pride filled the Corinthians in spite of the terrible sin in their midst.

Not mourned. The Corinthians should have mourned and had sorrow for the sin that was in front of them. The word for mourned means "to grieve (the feeling or the act):—mourn, (be-) wail."[7] Grief is the motive that should drive any action the church takes in dealing with this sinner. "In view of this,

---

[5] There is a question as to whether this verse refers to the father as the one who was wronged. If it is, it would suggest that he was still living at the time.
[6] Ketcherside, W. Carl, *A Clean Church*, 93.
[7] Strong, J. (2009). *A Concise Dictionary of the Words in the Greek Testament and The Hebrew Bible* (Vol. 1, p. 56). Bellingham, WA: Logos Bible Software.

we can well recognize that there are many congregations today which blatantly boast of their accomplishments, but which would be much more in character if they put on the sackcloth and ashes of deep grief at the sins which they have tolerated."[8]

Not taken him away. Their mourning and sorrow should have led to the action of taking him away. To "take him away" simply means to withdraw from him (cf. 2 Thess. 3:6). In verses 3-13, Paul gives detailed instruction concerning what "take him away" means and how.

The Instruction (vv. 3-13) – Put the Fornicator Away from You

No question about what should be done (vv. 3-4). Paul makes two points in these two verses. 1. *Paul had already concluded the obvious* (v. 3). As if he were present with the church, Paul made his decision about what the conclusion should be. The facts about the case cannot be denied.

2. *The authority of Christ tells us what to do* (v. 4). We are to take direction from the head of the church, which is Christ (Eph. 1:22). Christ endorses the action a church takes as long it acts in harmony with the revealed will. To ignore or rebel against the instructions on discipline is to reject the authority of Christ.

For the whole church (v. 4). Withdrawing is not the action of the elders only or a small part of the church. Rather, the whole church is involved. The phrase, "when you are gathered together" suggests that something is to take place in the assembly. Why would it be important to announce in the assembly that we are withdrawing from the brother who is identified? This action needs to be done so the rest may fear (cf. Acts 5:11; 1 Tim. 1:19-20). This enables and encourages all to make efforts to restore the wayward (Gal. 6:1). Furthermore, all will know with whom they are not to keep company and why (vv. 9-11).

Purpose for putting him away (vv. 6-8). These verses set forth a two-fold purpose. (1) *To save the erring* (v. 5). These brethren are told to "deliver such a one to Satan." There are two realms: the kingdom of God and the kingdom of Satan. This expression refers to identifying the realm in which the person

---
8   Ketcherside, W. Carl, *A Clean Church*, 95.

has chosen to live. Let him live that life and face the consequences thereof, but not be identified as a child of God at the same time.

Putting away is to be done "for the destruction of the flesh." That is, that the desires of the flesh would be destroyed. In other words, the sin might cease. Perhaps a parallel passage would be 1 Timothy 1:20 where Paul delivers Hymenaeus and Alexander to Satan "that they may learn not to blaspheme" (parallel to "destruction of the flesh"). The end goal is "that his spirit may be saved in the day of the Lord Jesus."

(2) *Maintain the purity of the church* (vv. 6-8). (a) To ignore the sin is to leave a leavening influence (v. 6). Even a small amount of leaven will leaven the whole lump. Thus, their glorying (cf. v. 2) is not good.

"Not infrequently does a group become so concerned about one issue that they measure faithfulness solely on the basis of that one issue. Faithfulness, to such persons, is not measured by the kind of life one is living but by where a person stands on a particular issue...Anytime a group tolerates any evil, its moral standards are lowered."[9]

(b) "Therefore purge out the old leaven" (v. 7). This alludes to the Passover Feast when the Jews were to put away all the leaven from the house for seven days (Ex. 12:1-19). Likewise, the sinner is to remove his sin (leaven) lest it corrupt the whole lump (the church). The phrase, "since you truly are unleavened" refers to their claim or profession of purity. "That is, as ye are bound by your Christian profession to be unleavened, or to be pure. Your very profession implies this, and you ought, therefore, to remove all impurity, and to become holy. Let there be no impurity, and no mixture inconsistent with that holiness which the gospel teaches and requires."[10]

"For indeed Christ, our Passover, was sacrificed for us" is given as a reason for the urgency of dealing with the sin in their midst. In Exodus 12, the leaven was removed prior to the sacrifice of the Passover lamb.

> The connection of this lamb with Paul's admonition is implied yet is evident and clear: the Passover Lamb slain, and the Passover

---

9   Mike Willis, *Commentary on 1 Corinthians*, 139-140.
10 Barnes, A. (1884–1885). *Notes on the New Testament: I Corinthians*. (R. Frew, Ed.) (p. 87). London: Blackie & Son.

Feast thus begun, and yet the old leaven not cleaned out of the house—what a contradiction! If such a thing would be frightful in the case of the Jews who slew and ate only lambs which were merely types, how much worse is it for us Christians who have our divine Lamb, the antitype, slain once for the deliverance of the world![11]

The point is, since our Passover lamb (Christ) has already been sacrificed, the church at Corinth was running late or behind on removing the leaven.

(c) The feast must be kept without compromise (v. 8). The feast is not to be kept with "malice and wickedness," that is with a "vicious disposition and evil deed."[12] The word for malice means "wickedness, depravity: 1 Co. 5:8… wickedness that is not ashamed to break the laws"[13] The word for wickedness "refers to the state of being wicked or evil." "In the NT, the word regularly refers to people being in a state of malice and sin, opposed to God and divine truth (Luke 11:39; 1 Cor. 5:8)."[14]

Rather, the feast is to be kept with "sincerity and truth," which seem to be just the opposite of malice and wickedness. The word for sincerity comes from a word that means "judged by sunlight, i.e. tested as genuine (fig.):—pure, sincere."[15] A. T. Robertson observes, "The Greek idea of truth is out in the open.[16] Vincent quotes Bengel as saying, "Sincerity takes care not to admit evil with the good; truth, not to admit evil instead of good."[17]

Not to company with him (vv. 9-11). These verses will be covered more thoroughly in lesson 7, but here they will be summarized for us to see the flow of the text.

---

11   Lenski, R. C. H. (1963). *The Interpretation of St. Paul's First and Second Epistle to the Corinthians* (p. 222). Minneapolis, MN: Augsburg Publishing House.
12   Robertson, A. T. (1933). *Word Pictures in the New Testament* (1 Co 5:1). Nashville, TN: Broadman Press.
13   Thayer, J. H. (1889). *A Greek-English Lexicon of the New Testament: Being Grimm's Wilke's Clavis Novi Testamenti* (p. 320). New York: Harper & Brothers.
14   Gleaves, G. S. (2014). Evil. D. Mangum, D. R. Brown, R. Klippenstein, & R. Hurst (Eds.), *Lexham Theological Wordbook*. Bellingham, WA: Lexham Press.
15   Strong, J. (2009). *A Concise Dictionary of the Words in the Greek Testament and The Hebrew Bible* (Vol. 1, p. 56). Bellingham, WA: Logos Bible Software.
16   Robertson, A. T. (1933). *Word Pictures in the New Testament* (1 Co 5:8). Nashville, TN: Broadman Press.
17   Vincent, M. R. (1887). *Word Studies in the New Testament* (Vol. 3, p. 211). New York: Charles Scribner's Sons.

Previous instructions explained (vv. 9-10). Paul says in a previous letter not to company (socialize) with fornicators (v. 9). The church at Corinth needed this instruction in a city given to immorality. However, they apparently thought he meant not to associate with *any* fornicator. Paul clarifies that he did not mean those of this world (v. 10). If so, one would need to go out of the world. What a sad commentary on society!

Do not company with a brother in sin (v. 11). If a brother continues in sin, do not company with him (v. 11a). Paul then enumerates a list of sinners saying, "sexually immoral, or covetous, or an idolater, or a reviler, or a drunkard, or an extortioner" (v. 11b). This list is not exhaustive, but representative of all sinners. There are some not mentioned here like murderers and liars. Should we withdraw from the extortioner and idolater, but not the murderer? Should we discipline the reviler but not the liar? Eating is one way to have "company," but it is not limited to that (vv. 11c).

Just those within the church (vv. 12-13a). We can and must judge those within the church (v. 12). Paul had already judged what should be done (cf. v. 3). God will judge those without (outside the church, v. 13a).

Put away the wicked person (v. 13b). This is the very thing they had not done (v. 2). The writer seems to borrow language from Moses (Deut. 13:5; 17:7, 12; 19:19; 21:21; 22:21, 24; 24:7). Some parallel expressions found in this chapter help us to understand putting away the wicked person: "taken away from among you" (v. 2), "deliver such a one to Satan" (v. 5), "purge out the old leaven" (v. 7), "not to keep company" (v. 11), and "not even to eat" (v. 11).

In the next lesson, we will focus on what "not to keep company" means and explore how the church reacted to these instructions.

Questions

1. How could Paul judge what should be done with the fornicator when he is not even present in Corinth? _____
_____
_____

2. How does the case of fornication at Corinth compare to the Gentile world? _____
_____

3. Why is the church "puffed up"? _____
_____
_____

4. What two reasons does Paul give suggesting there is no question about what should be done (vv. 3-4)? _____
_____
_____

5. What do we learn from the phrase "when you are gathered together" (v. 4)? _____
_____
_____

6. What does it mean to deliver one to Satan (v. 5)? _____
_____
_____

7. What does "for the destruction of the flesh" (v. 5) mean? _____
_____
_____

8. What is the point Paul makes by mentioning that Christ our Passover is sacrificed for us? _____
_____
_____

9. What is the contrast between malice and wickedness versus sincerity and truth? _____
_____
_____

10. How would you respond to the contention that the list of sins (or sinners) are the only ones we can discipline? _____
_____
_____
_____

The Case at Corinth (Part 2)

Lesson 7

We continue our study of the case at Corinth. What happened at Corinth beyond the instruction to withdraw in 1 Corinthians 5? Did they do what they were told? If they did, what impact did it have on the fornicator?

Review of the Instructions of 1 Corinthians 5

The problem (v. 1). The church at Corinth had a fornicator in their midst. The situation was well reported. It was a case where a man had taken his father's wife. Even the Gentiles did not tolerate such a situation.

The failure (v. 2). The church had not dealt with the fornicator properly. They were puffed up (filled with pride) in spite of the sin in the church. They should have been mourning but were not. They had not taken action to bring the sinner to repentance.

The instruction (vv. 3-13). The church was instructed to put the fornicator away from them. Paul said that there was no question about what should be done (vv. 3-4). The whole church was to take action (v. 4). The purpose of the discipline was to save the erring brother and keep the church pure (vv. 5-8). The instruction included not keeping company with the brother in sin (vv. 9-11). Paul said that the Christians at Corinth had the responsibility to judge those within the church (vv. 12-13a). He concluded by telling them to put away the wicked person (v. 13b).

The Meaning of "Company"

"Not to keep company." In our previous study, we only made passing reference to the meaning of "not to keep company" (1 Cor. 5:9, 11). Here we take a closer look.

Translations: The KJV, ASV, NKJV, MEV, and YLT use the word "company." It is rendered "associate" in the ESV, NASB, RSV, NIV, NET, NCV, and the footnote of the NKJV. The LBP (v. 9) has "not to mix with," as well as Darby's translation.

Defined: Strong's defines the word translated "company" as "*4874 from 4862 and a comp. of 303 and 3396;* to mix up together, i.e. (fig.) associate with:—(have, keep) company (with)."[1] Thayer says, "*to mix up together … to keep company with, be intimate with.*"[2]

Vincent comments, "The translation *company* is inadequate, but cannot perhaps be bettered. The word is compounded of σύν *together,* ἀνά *up and down among,* and μίνυμι *to mingle.* It denotes, therefore, not only close, but habitual, intercourse."[3] Lenski defines the word as, "mix yourselves—up—with."[4] Vine's says, "lit., 'to mix up with' (*sun,* 'with,' *ana,* 'up,' *mignumi,* 'to mix, mingle'), signifies 'to have, or keep, company with.'"[5]

Thus, to keep company refers to socializing—mixing up together with someone. Not keeping company is an essential and effective part of church discipline. "Church discipline is social ostracism; therefore it is effective or ineffective in direct proportion to how well the members personally disassociate themselves from the sinner."[6] That is exactly the point Paul is making in our text (1 Cor. 5:11). Quite often we are hoping and praying that some wayward member (including our own family or close friends) will turn back to the Lord, yet we continue to socialize with them all the while scratching our heads, wondering why they do not change.

"Not even to eat." This phrase is not referring to the Lord's Supper as some have supposed. How could the faithful keep the unfaithful from partaking of the Lord's Supper? The association forbidden here is permitted with the

---

1 Strong, J. (2009). *A Concise Dictionary of the Words in the Greek Testament and The Hebrew Bible* (Vol. 1, p. 68). Bellingham, WA: Logos Bible Software.
2 Thayer, J. H. (1889). *A Greek-English Lexicon of the New Testament: Being Grimm's Wilke's Clavis Novi Testamenti* (p. 601). New York: Harper & Brothers.
3 Vincent, M. R. (1887). *Word Studies in the New Testament* (Vol. 3, p. 211). New York: Charles Scribner's Sons.
4 Lenski, R. C. H. (1963). *The Interpretation of St. Paul's First and Second Epistle to the Corinthians* (p. 225). Minneapolis, MN: Augsburg Publishing House.
5 Vine, W. E., Unger, M. F., & White, W., Jr. (1996). *Vine's Complete Expository Dictionary of Old and New Testament Words* (Vol. 2, p. 116). Nashville, TN: T. Nelson.
6 Mike Willis, *Commentary on 1 Corinthians,* 144.

world (1 Cor. 5:10). Is that the Lord's Supper? The eating is part of "keeping company," thus, part of socializing (a common meal).

Eating is just one part of "company." Keeping company involves more than just eating. It is a general term of which eating is a part. It would include such things as social visits, shopping together, or playing games together. Eating is just one specific form of "company."

Some have the idea that "not even to eat" suggests that eating is all that is involved in keeping company. Some believe you may socialize with the withdrawn as much as you want, but eating is off limits. For example, if a brother has been withdrawn from, you may play golf with him all day, but you just cannot eat with him at the clubhouse between the ninth and tenth hole. Or, if a sister has been disciplined, another sister in the Lord may go shopping with her all day, go to a movie, but when she suggests stopping for dinner on the way home, the faithful sister must refuse saying, "I can't keep company with you." How absurd.

Perhaps one reason Paul mentions eating here is that it shows some degree of approval. Peter's refusal to eat with the Gentiles demonstrates that (Gal. 2:11-14).

Reaction to Instructions of 1 Corinthians 5

What we know about how the first letter was received, whether the church changed, and whether the fornicator repented depends upon whether 2 Corinthians 2 and 7 are referring to the first Corinthian letter. This writer takes the view that both chapters are pointing back to the first letter.

The church at Corinth changed. They took the proper action (2 Cor. 7). How the first letter would be received concerned Paul. Titus was the messenger who delivered the letter. Paul went to Troas hoping to meet up with him to learn of its reception. But, Titus did not show. So, he anxiously made his way to Macedonia to finally connect with him and learn of the reaction to his letter (2 Cor. 2:12-13).

Paul rejoiced to hear the report of Titus (vv. 6-7). Paul's first letter was hard or severe (2 Cor. 10:10). However, Titus reported that the letter was embraced and well received (vv. 6-7). When Titus told of their desire, mourning, and zeal, Paul rejoiced.

The first Corinthian letter produced repentance (vv. 8-12). The letter caused sorrow that led to repentance (vv. 8-10). Paul's letter had made them sorry, though just for a little while, because it made them change. Their repentance produced (v.11) diligence (action, promptness), clearing of themselves (getting something out of their hearts and lives), indignation (hatred toward sin), fear (awe and respect for God and being afraid of displeasing Him), vehement desire (longing to do right), zeal (enthusiasm, fire), and vindication (proving that you are clear of fault).

What a change! The very points mentioned in verse 11 were the very things missing when Paul wrote the first letter.

The discipline caused the fornicator to repent (2 Cor. 2). Does 2 Corinthians 2 refer to the fornicator of 1 Corinthians 5? Most students think that it does. Arguments that it does not are based on the assumption of a visit and a lost letter that came between the first and second Corinthian letters. Tertullian (one of the "church fathers") argues that it did not point back to the man in 1 Corinthians 5. This concept is based on the tears (2 Cor. 2:4) Paul shed while writing to them. The thought being it does not fit the first Corinthian letter.

> They fail to find the tears about which Paul speaks. They catalog the passages where Paul may have and where he could not have shed tears when he was dictating First Corinthians. The view that the whole letter must be dripping with tears, that all of the emotion of the writer must lie revealed on the surface, in fact, that his tears ought to be mentioned in the proper places where he had shed them is unwarranted.[7]
>
> And there is no sufficient ground in the passage for the assumption of an intermediate letter, or that there is here

---

7 Lenski, R. C. H. (1963). *The Interpretation of St. Paul's First and Second Epistle to the Corinthians* (p. 874-875). Minneapolis, MN: Augsburg Publishing House.

meant, not the unchaste person, but a slanderer rebuked by Paul in this intermediate letter.[8]

We are now ready for a word regarding the question as to whether Paul speaks about the case of incest that is known to us from 1 Cor. 5. Every detail of our paragraph (v. 5–11) not only corresponds with that case but cannot be understood if that case is not referred to. If 2 Cor. 2:5–11 does not speak about the case mentioned in 1 Cor. 5, we must invent a duplicate of that case (save only that it need not be a case of incest) which would otherwise have the same characteristics. The critics do that. They disregard 1 Cor. 5 and set up a hypothetical case that fits 2 Cor. 2:5–7 plus 7:12. The results have been confusing. Paul himself has made it impossible to substitute a hypothetical case. He does it in the simplest way by writing in such a manner that, unless one is acquainted with the actual case (1 Cor. 5), one cannot understand a number of the expressions which he employs in v. 5–11. First Corinthians 5 is so completely the key to 2 Cor. 2:5–11 that, when this key is disregarded, the door remains locked.[9]

Consider the following evidence that 2 Corinthians 2 refers to the case in 1 Corinthians 5. (1) This is a response to the first letter. Keep in mind that there is no substantial evidence of an intermediate letter. (2) Many or the majority punished the erring brother (v. 6). Compare that with the instructions about action to be taken in the assembly (1 Cor. 5:4). (3) This chapter (2 Cor. 2) addresses a specific person and not a general problem. That would well fit 1 Corinthians 5.

The discipline worked (2 Cor. 2). The church did what it should (v. 6). They took the action that they were instructed to take (1 Cor. 5). What they did worked. It brought him to repentance (vv. 6-7). Note the tenderness with which Paul dealt with the man. He never identified him by name or by his sin.

---

8 H.A.W. Meyer, *Critical and Exegetical Handbook on the Epistles to the Corinthians*, 443.
9 Lenski, R. C. H. (1963). *The Interpretation of St. Paul's First and Second Epistle to the Corinthians* (p. 892). Minneapolis, MN: Augsburg Publishing House.

The action taken was effective because of the group action (v. 6).[10] It is important now to forgive and comfort him (vv. 7-11). If not, he may be overcome with grief and be driven away or be rendered of little use in the church. The brethren are urged to reaffirm their love for him that he might be salvaged (v. 8). "At any rate, the time has come for tender love (agape) to supersede tough love."[11]

Some had evidently misunderstood and were not willing to accept him. Rather, they kept hammering him over his sin (vv. 10-11). Apparently, they refused to forgive. Perhaps the wide-ranging grief his sin had caused (v. 5) made it hard to forget. Coffman calls this spirit "super-piety."[12] What seems like a strong stand against sin may be a tool of Satan (v. 11). We can well see how that could happen today. When someone commits a heinous sin like adultery and then repents, it may be hard for some to forgive. They may think that those who now forgive and welcome him back with open arms are being "soft" on sin. The truth is this "strong stand" that cannot turn loose of the sin and embrace forgiveness is a device of Satan (v. 11).

Conclusions

There are four major points we want to take away from this lesson:

1. *Churches can change and begin withdrawing from a member who is not penitent.* At one congregation where I preached, church discipline had not been practiced in thirty years. A series of lessons on church discipline was preached and athe the end of the series two elders made a public acknowledgment. They led a prayer asking God to forgive them and the congregation. Their statement said that they were not responsible for the past thirty years, but only for the time they had been elders. They recognized that they could not undo the past or go back five, ten or more years and withdraw from those who should have been. All they knew to do was to repent, ask God to forgive, and start with present circumstances.

---

10 Some have concluded from the use of "majority" (NKJV) or "many" (KJV) that there was an element in the church that was sympathetic to the fornicator and refused to withdraw from him. That very well may have been the case (as is true in some churches today). It seems to this author that it is more a reference to the whole church dealing with him rather than just a few.
11 Melvin Curry, *The Book of 2 Corinthians*, 103.
12 James Burton Coffman, *Commentary on 1 and 2 Corinthians*, 323.

2. *Withdrawing works.* It always works because it pleases God and maintains the purity of the church. However, at Corinth, it went even further and brought the sinner back. When done properly, it does not drive one away; it brings him back.

3. *Not keeping company is an essential and effective part of discipline.* Withdrawing involves far more than announcing at services that we are taking disciplinary action against a brother or sister.

4. *Forgiving and receiving the penitent is just as important as withdrawing.*

Questions

1. Give a summary of the instructions that were given in 1 Corinthians 5.

2. What does it mean to "keep company"?

3. Does "not even to eat" refer to the Lord's Supper? Explain.

4. How did the church at Corinth receive the first Corinthian letter?

5. What impact did the first Corinthian letter have on the church and the action it was failing to take?

6. What evidence can be given that 2 Corinthians 2 is referring to the fornicator of 1 Corinthians 5? _____
_____
_____

7. What effect did church discipline have on the fornicator? _____
_____
_____

8. What device of Satan is alluded to in 2 Corinthians 2:11? _____
_____
_____

9. What four major points do we take away from this lesson? _____
_____
_____
_____

10. For class discussion, How did the action taken by the Corinthian church lead the fornicator to repentance when their toleration (acceptance) of him did not? _____
_____
_____
_____

The Case at Thessalonica

Lesson 8

The second notable case of discipline in the New Testament occurred in Thessalonica (2 Thess. 3) and the circumstance is different from that in Corinth. At Corinth, the discipline involved a moral issue. At Thessalonica, discipline involved two sins based on a misunderstanding of the second coming.

The Command to Withdraw (v. 6)

Command. Robertson observes, "Note of apostolic authority here, not advice or urging, but command."[1] "Its meaning is better understood when we note that it signifies 'to pass a military order along,' one that comes from a superior commander...."[2]

We would not think of ignoring other commands like baptism (Acts 2:38) or giving (1 Cor. 16:1-2). Why then, do some churches push aside this one as if it is nothing? If someone started to worship with a new congregation and found that they did not take up a collection, he would be disturbed. However, if he found that the same church had not withdrawn from anyone in years, he is not as bothered. To ignore or fail to practice church discipline is to disregard the command of God.

The command is given "in the name of Jesus." To do something "in the name" of Christ is to do it by the authority of Christ (cf. Acts 4:7). Christ has all authority (Matt. 28:18). He is the head of the church (Col. 1:18). Thus,

---

1 Robertson, A. T. (1933). *Word Pictures in the New Testament* (2 Th 3:4). Nashville, TN: Broadman Press.
2 Lenski, R. C. H. (1937). *The Interpretation of St. Paul's Epistles to the Colossians, to the Thessalonians, to Timothy, to Titus and to Philemon* (p. 453). Columbus, OH: Lutheran Book Concern.

the command to withdraw is given by the authority of Christ. Paul makes the same point to the Corinthians (1 Cor. 5:4).

Withdraw. Thayer defines the word for withdraw as "*to bring together, contract, shorten ... to diminish, check, cause to cease; pass. to cease to exist: ... to remove one's self, withdraw one's self, to depart, ... to abstain from familiar intercourse with one,* 2 Th. 3:6."[3] Vine says it means "'to bring together, gather up' (used of furling sails), hence, in the middle voice, signifies 'to shrink from a person or thing,' 2 Thess. 3:6, 'withdraw'; elsewhere, 2 Cor. 8:20, 'avoiding.'"[4] Hence, it is the idea of pulling back, abstaining, avoiding, or removing. What this involves, including the details and how, is developed later in the text.

Some parallel statements in 1 Corinthians 5 help us understand what "withdraw" means: "taken away from among you" (v. 2), "deliver such a one to Satan" (v. 5), "purge out the old leaven" (v. 7), and "put away from yourselves that evil person" (v. 13).

Withdrawing involves action on the part of the church and the individual. For the church, the action is public—in the assembly (1 Cor. 5:4; 2 Cor. 2:6; 2 Thess. 3:6). For the individual, there are social restrictions—not to keep company (2 Thess. 3:14).

Every brother. The phrase "every brother" means any and all who walk disorderly, including family and close friends. To heed this passage means churches will be consistent in the practice of discipline. Partiality is eliminated (1 Tim. 5:21).

Walks disorderly.[5] The word translated "disorderly" (*atakōs*) is a military term meaning not keeping rank. W. E. Vine defines the word:

A. *Adjective.*
>   *atakos* (ἄτακτος, 813) signifies "not keeping order" (*a*, negative, *tasso*, "to put in order, arrange"); it was especially

---

[3] Thayer, J. H. (1889). *A Greek-English lexicon of the New Testament: Being Grimm's Wilke's Clavis Novi Testamenti* (p. 587). New York: Harper & Brothers.
[4] Vine, W. E., Unger, M. F., & White, W., Jr. (1996). *Vine's Complete Expository Dictionary of Old and New Testament Words* (Vol. 2, p. 680). Nashville, TN: T. Nelson.
[5] Go back to lesson 5 for a previous discussion about the word "disorderly." The points here that define the term are repeated from lesson 5.

a military term, denoting "not keeping rank, insubordinate"; it is used in 1 Thess. 5:14, describing certain church members who manifested an insubordinate spirit, whether by excitability or officiousness or idleness. See UNRULY.¶

B. *Adverb.*

ataktos (ἀτάκτως, 814) signifies "disorderly, with slackness" (like soldiers not keeping rank) 2 Thess. 3:6; in v. 11 it is said of those in the church who refused to work, and became busybodies (cf. 1 Tim. 5:13).¶

C. *Verb.*

atakteo (ἀτακτέω, 812) signifies "to be out of rank, out of one's place, undisciplined, to behave disorderly": in the military sense, "to break rank"; negatively in 2 Thess. 3:7, of the example set by the apostle and his fellow missionaries, in working for their bread while they were at Thessalonica so as not to burden the saints. See BEHAVE.¶[6]

Thayer defines the word, "ἄ-τακτος, -ον, (τάσσω), d*isorderly, out of the ranks*, (often so of soldiers); .... *deviating from the prescribed order or rule*: 1 Th. 5:14, cf. 2 Th. 3:6." [7]

Albert Barnes observes, "A 'disorderly walk' denotes conduct that is in any way contrary to the rules of Christ. The proper idea of the word used here (ἀτάκτως), is that of soldiers who do not keep the ranks; who are regardless of order; and then who are irregular in any way. The word would include any violation of the rules of Christ on any subject."[8]

The same word is translated "unruly." "Now we exhort you, brethren, warn those who are *unruly*, comfort the fainthearted, uphold the weak, be patient with all" (1 Thess. 5:14, emphasis mine DVR). This text also mentions the fainthearted (discouraged) and the weak as being different than the

---

[6] Vine, W. E., Unger, M. F., & White, W., Jr. (1996). *Vine's Complete Expository Dictionary of Old and New Testament Words* (Vol. 2, p. 680). Nashville, TN: T. Nelson.

[7] Thayer, J. H. (1889). *A Greek-English lexicon of the New Testament: Being Grimm's Wilke's Clavis Novi Testamenti* (p. 83). New York: Harper & Brothers.

[8] Barnes, A. (1884–1885). *Notes on the New Testament: I Thessalonians to Philemon.* (R. Frew, Ed.) (p. 99). London: Blackie & Son.

unruly. Thus, we learn that the disorderly (unruly) are not the same as being fainthearted or weak.

The context of 2 Thessalonians 3:6 helps us understand how the word disorderly is used. First, he "walks" disorderly suggesting a continuance in the disorderly conduct (v. 6). His behavior is not according to the tradition of the apostles (v. 6). Neither is he obeying the word of the epistle (v. 14).

The Sins to Be Addressed (vv. 7-12)

There are two sins in this context that came from a misunderstanding of the second coming. The error involved the idea that the second coming was imminent (2 Thess. 2:1-3). One sin was laziness. Apparently, some had quit working since they thought Christ was about to return (2 Thess. 3:7-12). The second sin, becoming a busybody, may have resulted from the previous sin of laziness (2 Thess. 3:11-12).

"The fact that a rather lengthy paragraph (verses 6-15) is devoted to this sin would seem to indicate that the evil here signalized had grown worse since the first epistle was written (see on 1 Thess. 4:11, 12; 5:14; then also 1 Thess. 2:9)."[9]

Lazy. This conduct was not according to the example of Paul and his companions (vv. 7-9). They were not lazy but worked while they were in their midst. They did not eat at the burden of others. Paul and his fellow-laborers could have demanded support but did not so that they might be an example to the brethren (v. 9).

Those that do not work should not eat (v. 10). Paul instructs them not to help the lazy. It is not inhumane or inconsiderate to refuse to aid those who will not work.

Laziness is disorderly conduct (v. 11). Paul labels this conduct as that which is a step out of rank.

The apostle gives a command to work (v. 12). Christ commands us to work. In so doing, the Thessalonians would eat their bread and not that of others.

---

9   William Hendriksen, *New Testament Commentary, Exposition of I and II Thessalonians*, 199.

Busybodies. Being a busybody is disorderly conduct (v. 11). Apparently, previous instructions about minding their own business (1 Thess. 4:11) had gone unheeded. Thus, continuing in the sin suggests a walk that is disorderly.

What does "busybody" mean? The NET translates this, "meddling in the work of others." The NCV renders this, "busy themselves in other people's lives." The LBP simply has "gossiping." Lenski comments, "The latter means to be busy with what is none of their business."[10] Vine's defines the word as, "lit., 'to be working round about, instead of at one's own business' (*peri*, 'around,' *ergon*, 'work'), signifies to take more pains than enough about a thing, to waste one's labor, to be meddling with, or bustling about, other people's matters." "This may be produced in a free rendering: 'some who are not busied in their own business, but are overbusied in that of others.'"[11]

Paul commanded them to work with quietness (v. 12), which is the opposite to being a busybody.

The Attitude That Is Essential (v. 13)

The apostle adds, "But as for you, brethren, do no grow weary in doing good." The NCV says, "never become tired of doing good."

General principle. Not growing weary is a general principle taught throughout the New Testament (Gal. 6:9; Luke 18:1). The point is that we should not be discouraged when we are doing what is right. "Do not be misled. Do not let a few people who neglect their duty keep you from doing yours. Never grow tired of doing what is right, honorable, excellent."[12] The context would include, but not be limited to helping those who need help (cf. v. 10), and working quietly and eating your bread (v. 12). One could become discouraged as he works to feed his own family and as he helps those who are in need, only to find some who are lazy and abuse the generosity that had been given. It may be tempting just to quit helping others at all.

---

10   Lenski, R. C. H. (1937). *The Interpretation of St. Paul's Epistles to the Colossians, to the Thessalonians, to Timothy, to Titus and to Philemon* (p. 463). Columbus, OH: Lutheran Book Concern.
11   Vine, W. E., Unger, M. F., & White, W., Jr. (1996). *Vine's Complete Expository Dictionary of Old and New Testament Words* (Vol. 2, p. 85). Nashville, TN: T. Nelson.
12   William Hendriksen, *New Testament Commentary, Exposition of I and II Thessalonians*, 204.

It will apply to taking disciplinary action. "To this we are able to assent, only with the remark, that we understand the phrase as comprehensively as possible—as including, therefore, both their own unblameable walk, steady, loving, earnest discipline (vv. 14, 15), and also a due beneficence."[13] This certainly fits the thrust of the context. The verses before and after are dealing with taking disciplinary action. In withdrawing, we must not give up or be discouraged: we are doing what is right. We are pleasing God. We are doing what is best for the church. We are doing what is best for the erring. We are doing what is best for our families. We are doing what is best for our souls.

The Instructions to Follow (vv. 14-15)

Note that person. "The first step is to discriminate between those who obeyed and those who did not. The second was to note him as disobedient."[14] The word "note" means "Lit. set a mark on. The nature of the mark is indicated in the next clause."[15] He is to be identified for the purpose of withdrawing (See v. 6). At Corinth, something was to be said and done in the assembly (1 Cor. 5:4).

Not keep company with him. This is the same expression and meaning as found in 1 Corinthians 5:9, 11.[16] The word "company" means "to mix up together."[17] It is the idea of associating or socializing.

The reason given is "that he may be ashamed." It is to bring him to penitent shame and win him back to the Lord. This would be parallel to "that his spirit may be saved" (1 Cor. 5:5). "The shame will probably result when the individual in question begins to reflect on the patient and loving manner in which, in spite of his own grievous error which is pointed out to him (see verse 15), this 'discipline' is being exercised."[18]

---

13 Lange, J. P., Schaff, P., Auberlen, C. A., Riggenbach, C. J., & Lillie, J. (2008). *A Commentary on the Holy Scriptures: 1 & 2 Thessalonians* (p. 157). Bellingham, WA: Logos Bible Software.
14 David Lipscomb, *A Commentary on the New Testament Epistles: I, II Thessalonians, I, II Timothy, Titus, Philemon,* 112.
15 Vincent, M. R. (1887). *Word Studies in the New Testament* (Vol. 4, p. 71). New York: Charles Scribner's Sons.
16 Go back and review lesson 7 for more details of the meaning of "not keep company."
17 Thayer, J. H. (1889). *A Greek-English lexicon of the New Testament: Being Grimm's Wilke's Clavis Novi Testamenti* (p. 601). New York: Harper & Brothers.
18 William Hendriksen, *New Testament Commentary, Exposition of I and II Thessalonians,* 206.

A friend of mine, who is a preacher, recently related an experience he had which illustrates this point. He had recently moved to a different congregation where he and his wife did not know all the people or those who the congregation had withdrawn from in the past. One Sunday when some of the brethren were planning a potluck (or pitch-in) meal, the preacher's wife invited some visitors to come (not knowing the church had withdrawn from the woman sometime before). The preacher and his wife realized their mistake before they got to the dinner. In a little while, the couple drove up and got out with the food they had picked up on the way.

Some of the elders met them outside and explained that the invitation was innocent, but they would need to leave because the brethren could not keep company with them until she repented. The couple got mad and left. The meal was ruined for everyone.

When the preacher got home his phone was ringing off the wall—it was the couple that got mad, and they were steaming. The preacher and his wife immediately drove over to see them. The plan was just to let the couple blow off steam and calm down before making any attempt at reasoning with them. So, the couple let loose about how the church had treated them. The preacher and his wife just let them talk and apologized for inviting them without knowing the situation. Finally they began to reason from the Scriptures about why the church treated them the way it did. This discussion went on all Sunday afternoon. Time was closing in on the evening worship. So, the preacher asked if they could come back after services and continue the discussion. The couple agreed.

When the preacher got up to preach that night, he noticed the couple had come and were sitting in the back. When the congregation sang the invitation song, the couple responded and corrected their lives (she was restored, and he was baptized). What brought that about their response? Was it the fact that this church followed the teaching of 1 Corinthians 5 and 2 Thessalonians 3 about not keeping company? Had they all welcomed them to the dinner would a change have occurred?

Not treat him as an enemy. How the church treats the disorderly is not done in bitterness or retaliation. He is not our enemy, but our brother. Love and concern should drive our actions. We should not turn our backs on him as if he is hopeless.

Admonish him as a brother. Treat him as a family member you love. Admonish, encourage ("warn" ESV) him to correct his life. We should continue to admonish him after the withdrawal has taken place.

Questions

1. Define the word "withdraw." _____
   _____
   _____

2. What does the phrase "every brother" (v. 6) imply about the practice of withdrawing? _____
   _____
   _____

3. What does "disorderly" mean? _____
   _____
   _____

4. What was the misunderstanding about the second coming and how did it contribute to the sins that are addressed in our study? _____
   _____
   _____

5. According to verse 9, what did Paul and his companions have the right to do, but did not? Why did he not exercise his right? _____
   _____
   _____
   _____

6. What is the principle found in verse 13 and how does it relate to church discipline? _____
   _____
   _____

7. What does it mean to "note" the person (v. 14)? _____
_____
_____
_____

8. What does "keep company" mean? _____
_____
_____

9. What reason is given for not keeping company with those from whom we have withdrawn? _____
_____
_____
_____

10. How is the disciplined one to be treated and what does that mean? ___
_____
_____
_____
_____

How to Treat Those Disfellowshipped

Lesson 9

This lesson focuses on the two extremes of how to deal with those who have been disfellowshipped. One view is that we treat them like nothing is wrong—the same as we did before they became unfaithful. The other view is that we treat them like they have some disease and completely avoid them. Between those extremes are several misunderstandings.

When discipline fails, it is often because some of the members disregard Bible instructions on how to treat those who have been disciplined.

As we pursue answers to this question, let us not forget that discipline is to save the erring. Thus, the question is: "What is best for the erring?" How we treat the erring after withdrawal can make a world of difference concerning their return to the faith.

Who Should Withdraw from the Disorderly?

The whole church. The Corinthians were instructed to deal with the fornicator "when you are gathered together" (1 Cor. 5:4)—that is in the assembly of the whole church. When they took action against him, it was "punishment which was inflicted by the majority" (2 Cor. 2:6). It is not just the elders, the men, or a core element of the church that withdraws, but the whole congregation.

Since the whole church is expected to agree and support the discipline, they are entitled to know the facts of the case. Think of the power with the involvement of the entire church. What if every member were working toward restoring the erring (Gal. 6:1)? What if every single member made contact with the erring before a church withdraws? Then, after discipline has taken place, think of the impact if every member periodically contacts the erring. Think of the impact this would have!

Backed, supported, and upheld by all. Often, there is an element (at times sizeable) that does not support withdrawal which renders it ineffective. When one does not support church discipline, the following principles are true.[1]

(1) That person does not respect the authority of Christ.
(2) That person does not love the erring individual as he should.
(3) That person is not interested in keeping the church pure.
(4) That person is not interested in maintaining the respect of the world.
(5) That person must feel that the other members of the congregation need no example or warning.

The point is this: Since withdrawing is the action of the whole church, then how each member treats the withdrawn is very important.

How Should We Treat the Disorderly?

Principles. Let's consider some Bible principles (some of which we have already seen in the previous lessons) that govern how we treat those who have been disciplined and then make application of them.

1. *Demonstrate that you are trying to save the disorderly (Matt. 18:15-17).* Long before it reaches the point of church action, our communication with the wayward brother should make it obvious to him that we are trying to "gain" him.

2. *Treat the disorderly as a heathen and a publican (Matt. 18:17).* That is, deal with him as one living a wicked life. Do not do anything to show approval of his manner of life. Let him know that he is viewed in the same class as one outside the fold of God.

3. *Avoid the disorderly (Rom. 16:17).* This cannot mean that we totally avoid him (not even to speak to him) for we are to admonish him (2 Thess. 3:15). The word translated "avoid" literally means to "turn aside."[2] The same

---
1   These five points are taken from Royce DeBerry, *Church Discipline*, 60.
2   Vincent, M. R. (1887). *Word studies in the New Testament* (Vol. 3, p. 181). New York: Charles Scribner's Sons.

word is translated "turned aside" in Romans 3:12 and "turned away" in 1 Peter 3:11. The ASV translates our text as, "turn away from them." The point is: do not associate with them. Do not socialize. Do not be under their influence.

4. *Do not associate (1 Cor. 5:9, 11; 2 Thess. 3:14).* The word "company" means "to mix up together."³ We are not to socialize—not even to eat (1 Cor. 5:11).⁴ The design of this is to bring them to shame (2 Thess. 3:14).

5. *Do not treat the disorderly as an enemy, but admonish him as a brother (2 Thess. 3:15).* He is not to be forgotten. He is not to be treated as some unwanted relative. He is not to be viewed as our bitter enemy. Rather, deal with him as a brother (in error) whom we love and for whom we have the greatest care.

6. *Love the disorderly (2 Cor. 2:8).* When the fornicator returned to the Lord, Paul urged the church to "reaffirm your love to him." This verse implies that they had (or at least should have had) love for him before he returned. Love, in this case, is agape love that seeks the best for him (in this case – his salvation). The *agape* form of love means we treat him in a way that shows we love and care about him. This love does not necessarily involve feelings. "Christian love, whether exercised toward the brethren, or toward men generally, is not an impulse from the feelings, it does not always run with the natural inclinations, nor does it spend itself only upon those for whom some affinity is discovered. Love seeks the welfare of all..."⁵

7. *Be kind to the disorderly (Eph. 4:32).* Pulpit Commentary suggests that kindness is "sweet, amiable in disposition, subduing all that is harsh and hasty, encouraging all that is gentle and good..."⁶ Dealing with the erring does not mean we need to be ugly or rude. We can rebuke and at the same time be kind.

---

3   Thayer, J. H. (1889). *A Greek-English lexicon of the New Testament: Being Grimm's Wilke's Clavis Novi Testamenti* (p. 601). New York: Harper & Brothers.
4   For more details on the meaning of "company" look back to lesson 7.
5   Vine, W. E., Unger, M. F., & White, W., Jr. (1996). *Vine's Complete Expository Dictionary of Old and New Testament Words* (Vol. 2, p. 382). Nashville, TN: T. Nelson.
6   Spence-Jones, H. D. M. (Ed.). (1909). *Ephesians* (p. 154). London; New York: Funk & Wagnalls Company.

8. *Seek to restore (Gal. 6:1).* Attempts to restore should be done both before and after withdrawing. We should continue to look for and use opportunities to talk with the erring about his soul. Every member should be involved in such efforts.

At times when a church is ready to withdraw from some erring member, some may think more should have been done before reaching this point. When one feels that enough has not been done, encourage him to do more individually to help the erring one..

9. *Demonstrate a willingness to forgive.* This principle is implied in Matthew 18:15-17. With every step, approaching the disorderly should be with the goal of gaining him back, thus a willingness to forgive. Paul's instruction to the church at Corinth says they should forgive, comfort, and reaffirm their love (2 Cor. 2:6-8). We should not rebuke the erring with an attitude of "I'm glad I have a reason to condemn you..."

Application. Let's take the principles that we have just considered and see how they apply in everyday circumstances. The questions to be answered are: Does my action violate any of these principles? Does what I want to do harmonize with these Bible principles? Am I making sure that nothing violates my conscience (Rom. 14:23)?

Situation: Suppose you run into one from whom the church has withdrawn at the grocery or the mall. Should you seek to avoid him? Do you refuse to speak? Do you avoid eye contact? The principles above are not violated by speaking to him. In fact, the principle of love, kindness, and not treating him as an enemy says we should not run from or avoid any contact with this brother.

Situation: Suppose someone invites you to a social setting where one who has been disciplined is in attendance. Do you stay lest you hurt someone's feelings? Do you leave? Staying violates the principle of not keeping company (1 Cor. 5:9, 11; 2 Thess. 3:14). Leaving does not mean you need to be rude. It is in circumstances like this where the "rubber meets the road." The principles we are considering are not just theory.

Situation: Suppose one who has been disciplined shows up at a social gathering. Suppose it is a potluck (pitch-in) dinner. Should those in charge ask him to leave? If it were at your house, should you invite him to stay? In our previous lesson, we related a story where this very thing happened. In fact, this has occurred in several places. While we want to be kind, we must follow the principle that we are not to keep company (not even to eat). Thus, those in charge of the social gathering should ask him to leave. As an elder and preacher, it would be necessary for me to kindly request the disciplined brother to leave the potluck or my house. As an elder (though elders are not overseeing social affairs but are leaders in the church), I would tell the disciplined brother who showed up at a potluck (or pitch-in) that they needed to leave.

Situation: What if one from whom we have withdrawn shows up at services? Do we ask him to leave? Do we show him he is unwanted? Do we ignore him, lest he feel welcome? Do we welcome him and tell him we are glad he came? What principle is violated by his attending services? In fact, we would want him to come. We would want any sinner—the adulterer, homosexual, drunkard, etc. to come. The congreation should welcome him. That does not mean we can socialize or eat with him.

Situation: What if you have some business dealings with the disciplined? What if the merchant where you shop is one that has been disfellowshipped? Suppose the new waitress at the restaurant that comes to serve you is a woman from whom the church has withdrawn? What if the serviceman that comes to repair your appliances is a man that has been disciplined? Or, what if the sales clerk that walks onto the floor to assist you is one from whom the church has withdrawn? Should you leave? Should you refuse the service? The truth of the matter is that none of the principles we have noticed are violated by some business contact with the disciplined. Some brethren do not have business dealings with one who has been disciplined because it violates their conscience. If that is the case, he should not violate his conscience (Rom. 14:23). That does not mean that others are doing wrong when they do have business dealings with the disorderly.

Situation: Suppose the disciplined REPENTS. Now, we are with him in a social setting a short time later. How should you treat him? Should you try to avoid him to show the disgust you have for what he did? Should you let him know it is tough for you to get over the heinous sin (i.e. adultery) that he committed? Should you speak and be kind, but try to distance yourself? Should you seek to give him a wholehearted embrace? This is the very thing that was addressed at Corinth (2 Cor. 2). Now that the fornicator had repented, they are told to forgive, comfort, and reaffirm their love. Thus, in the situation we have described, the proper action would be to give him a wholehearted embrace.

How we treat those who have been disciplined will have everything to do with the success or failure of our efforts to save them.

Questions

1. What are the extreme views that demand such a study as this lesson?

2. How is the whole church to be involved in church discipline?

3. Why is it important that the whole church be involved in church discipline?

4. How can one demonstrate that his efforts are trying to save the erring?

5. What does it mean to let one be as a "heathen and a publican" to you (Matt. 18:17)?

6. In what sense are we to "avoid" one who causes problems in the church (Rom 16:17? _____
_____
_____

7. How can we balance the principle of love and at the same time refuse to socialize with one who has been disciplined? _____
_____
_____

8. What should you do if you run into one from whom the church has withdrawn at the grocery or the mall? Should you avoid him? Should you speak to him? _____
_____
_____

9. What should you do if one who has been disciplined shows up at a social gathering? Should you stay lest feelings be hurt? Should you leave? _____
_____
_____

10. What should be done if one who has been disciplined shows up at services? _____
_____
_____
_____

Does It Apply to Family?

Lesson 10

Withdrawal from the disorderly is never pleasant. In fact, it should be a time of sadness (1 Cor. 5:1-2). That is especially true if it involves someone in your family.

Do the requirements of the text still apply even though it includes a family member? What if it is a brother, sister, son, or daughter? Can you continue with family activities? Can you associate at family gatherings? If families continue such association, will this bring the erring back?

Let's consider what the Bible says and how it applies to families.

The Standard

On any issue, especially one that is controversial, the problem often centers around what standard is used to settle the question.

Not emotions. Withdrawing is an emotional issue because of family ties.

There are other issues involving emotion. The difficulty is not in understanding the text, the definition of some word, or a translation problem. The difficulty is because of human situations that cry out for favor from the word of God. Divorce and remarriage is such an issue. The problem is not understanding Matthew 19:9. What makes it hard is when someone realizes, "That means that my daughter is living in adultery..."

The same is true for the issue of baptism. There is no problem understanding Mark 16:16. It becomes difficult when one realizes there is a discrepancy between what the text says and what their mother did before she died.

Man is not at liberty to decide for himself what is right. "Oh Lord, I know the way of man is not in himself; It is not in man who walks to direct his own steps" (Jer. 10:23). God's ways and thoughts are higher than man's ways and thoughts (Isa. 55:8-9). "There is a way that seems right to a man, But its end is the way of death" (Prov. 16:25). We must trust the Lord and not our own understanding (Prov. 3:5-6).

It is possible to let our emotions be the authority. We could easily become satisfied with our belief and practice, and thus be lost. Some will be deluded and believe a lie and be condemned (2 Thess. 2:10-12).

There are some things in God's word that do not seem fair and right. That is, using mere human reasoning, they do not seem fair, though they are. Asking Abraham to sacrifice his son does not seem fair and right (Gen 22). Neither does demanding those in the post-exile period leave their pagan wives and their children seem fair (Ezra 10:10-11, 44).

Not family. Often, family becomes the standard. Some have changed their views on divorce and remarriage to fit their son or daughter's situation. That makes family the standard. Another cannot accept baptism or membership in the one church as essential to salvation because that does not fit what their mother or grandmother did. Again, that makes family the standard. Concerning the issue we are addressing, some will determine how the disorderly should be treated based upon the family situation.

We must love the Lord more than family (Luke 14:26; Matt. 10:37). When we allow our family to be our standard, we love them more than God.

Following the Lord can bring rifts within families. Jesus said, "Do not think that I came to bring peace on earth. I did not come to bring peace but a sword. For I have come to 'set a man against his father, a daughter against her mother, and a daughter-in-law against her mother-in-law'; and 'a man's enemies will be those of his own household'" (Matt. 10:34-36).

We cannot show respect of persons (1 Tim. 5:21; James 2:1-9).

Word of God. Our standard must be the oracles of God (1 Pet. 4:11), what is written of God (2 Cor. 4:13), and the doctrine of Christ (2 John 9). If one has faith, he will accept what the Bible teaches because the Lord said it. Not because it fits what we want—it may not. Not because it fits our preconceived idea—it may not. Not because it is what we have always believed—it may not be. Not because it fits our family circumstance—it may not.

We cannot add to or take from the word (Rev. 22:18-19).

The Principles

So we can make application, it is helpful here to list three principles that we have already learned in previous studies.

We are to withdraw from the disorderly (2 Thess. 3:6).

The purpose of withdrawing is two-fold. The purpose is not to be mean, to be ugly, or to humiliate. One purpose is to *save the erring* (1 Cor. 5:5; 2 Thess. 3:14). The other purpose is to *maintain the purity of the church* (1 Cor. 5:6-8). Anything we do that offsets the impact of withdrawal also offsets the purposes of it.

Part of the disciplinary action is to not keep company with the one who is disorderly (1 Cor. 5:9, 11; 2 Thess. 3:14).

The Obligations

The Bible does not give contradictory commands. For example, we are commanded to work and provide for our families (1 Tim. 5:8; Eph. 4:28; 2 Thess. 3:10). We are also commanded to worship and not forsake the assembling of the saints (Heb. 10:25). Those are not contradictory. It is not a matter of disobeying one command to fulfill another. We can obey both. It is not an either-or choice.

There are family obligations that must be met. A husband and wife must fulfill the conjugal rights (1 Cor. 7:3-5). They have the duty to dwell together (1 Pet 3:7). Parents of a minor child have the responsibility to provide for him and continue to train him in the right way (1 Tim. 5:8; Eph. 6:1-4). Children are to honor their parents by providing for them when they are in need (1 Tim. 5:1-16). To refuse to associate at all in these cases would violate these commands.

The Family

Let's consider why the principles of withdrawal must apply to family.

We are to withdraw from "every brother" who is disorderly (2 Thess. 3:6). That includes family and close friends. If not, why not? The instructions to withdraw include not keeping company (v. 14). If the social restriction does not apply to family, does the withdrawing apply at all to one's family? If your relative walks disorderly would you want the church to withdraw from him? Would you want others (that are not family) to not keep company with him? Why? Would it be your hope that by others not associating with him, he might be brought to repentance?

No exceptions given. We must acknowledge there are exceptions to some of God's rules. For example, the rule is no divorce (Matt. 19:3-6; 1 Cor. 7:10-13). There is one exception: when it is for the cause of fornication (Matt. 19:9). The rule is that we are to obey the civil law (Rom. 13:1-7). There is the exception—when there is a conflict with obeying God (Acts 5:29). The rule is a Christian is not to go to law with another Christian (1 Cor. 6). There is the exception—when a Christian takes their unfaithful mate to court for divorce (Matt. 19:9). The family obligations (noted above) are required because we have passages that demand those obligations.

Command: Withdraw from Disorderly (Included: not to keep company)	
Have to Continue to Have a Close Association	**No Requirement to Have a Close Association**
Husband – Wife (1 Cor. 7:3-5)	Grown Child (No Passage)
Parent – Minor Child (Eph. 6:1-4)	Sibling (No Passage)
Care for Parent (1 Tim. 5:1-16)	Other Relatives (No Passage)

It is a stretch to say that grown children, siblings, aunts, uncles, nephews, nieces, etc. are exceptions. There are no passages requiring social contact in those cases.

In the Old Testament when those who led others to idolatry were to *be killed, a person's family was not exempt (Deut. 13:1-11).* That had to be hard. Go back and read that passage carefully and then ask yourself if you can honestly say, "I don't think God expects me not to associate with family."

Would the following events change the instructions? Would a wedding reception, holiday gathering (Thanksgiving, Christmas), family reunion, or birthday celebration?

If it does not apply to family, where does it stop with family? Does it extend to aunts, uncles, cousins, second cousins, or distant relatives? Would close friends be exempt as well? If not, why not?

There is to be no respect of persons. God is not a respecter of persons (Rom 2:11). We are not to show partiality either (James 2:1-9). If I refuse to associate with your relative who is disorderly, yet associate with mine, how am I not a respecter of persons?

Family and close friends will have the greatest impact. Not keeping company is designed to put pressure on the erring (1 Cor. 5:9, 11; 2 Thess. 3:14). Who will have the greatest impact—those closest to the disorderly or those who have little association anyway? When a congregation withdraws from one, and another member, who rarely associates with the one withdrawn, obeys the command to "not keep company," what impact does that have? However, when parents, children, siblings, and close friends obey the command to "not keep company" with the disorderly, what impact does that have? It WILL have an impact!

It is likely that there will be a time that you will be forced to make a decision about someone in your family. Many of us already have faced those times. Should you decide that you can associate and socialize, you will be practicing something that cannot be proved by the Word of God.

Should you decide to associate, do not put others in a compromising position. There have been some who conclude that since it is their family, they can associate with the erring. So, they have a gathering at their house and invite several brethren and include the erring relative too. That puts the others in a position to either violate their conscience or have to leave.

Should you decide to associate, YOU may be the very person that keeps your erring relative from returning to the Lord.

Questions

1. Why is it important to focus on the standard of authority in this lesson?
   _____
   _____
   _____

2. How is emotion used as a standard in dealing with this issue? _____
   _____
   _____

3. How is family used as a standard in dealing with this issue? _____
   _____
   _____

4. Considering the question of whether discipline applies to family, what three principles must be remembered? _____
   _____
   _____
   _____

5. List the family obligations that must be met even though those family members may be disciplined. _____
   _____
   _____

6. Who is included in "every brother" (2 Thess. 3:6)? _____
   _____
   _____

7. How would you respond to the contention that since a husband or wife must continue to have a relationship (in spite of withdrawal), then parents can have a continual social relationship with their grown child?

8. When church discipline is applied, who has the greatest impact on the erring and why? _____

9. If one decides they will associate with their family that has been disciplined and asks if you can give him assurance he is doing the right thing, what would you say? _____

10. How is the one who chooses to associate with their family that has been disciplined the very reason the erring does not repent? _____

Can We Withdraw from the Withdrawn?

Lesson 11

The question before us is, "Can the church withdraw from those who have withdrawn themselves?" By "withdrawn," we mean those who have quit assembling—they no longer attend. Good brethren disagree on this subject. Some argue that a church cannot withdraw from one who has withdrawn himself because "there is nothing to withdraw" they say.

We affirm that we can and should withdraw from those who no longer attend.

One Who Quits Is Walking Disorderly

"Disorderly" includes forsaking the assembling. The Thessalonians are told to withdraw from those who walk "disorderly" (2 Thess. 3:6). Thayer defines the word, "*out of the ranks*, (often so of soldiers); ... *deviating from the prescribed order or rule*: 1 Th. 5:14, cf. 2 Th. 3:6."[1]

Disorderly involves or includes one who "does not obey our word in this epistle" (2 Thess. 3:14). The epistle teaches, "stand fast and hold the traditions which you were taught, whether by word or our epistle" (2:15). Would that not include being faithful in attendance? We conclude that "disorderly" would include unfaithfulness in attendance (Heb. 10:25). Otherwise, we have at least one sin with which we cannot deal.

A general principle with specific application. In 2 Thessalonians 3 and 1 Corinthians 5, we have general principles with specific applications within the context. There are more applications to be made. Let's consider some parallels.

---

1   Thayer, J. H. (1889). *A Greek-English lexicon of the New Testament: Being Grimm's Wilke's Clavis Novi Testamenti* (p. 83). New York: Harper & Brothers.

In 2 John 4-11, there is the warning about not abiding in the doctrine of Christ (v. 9). One specific application is the denial of Christ (v. 7). Certainly, that would not be the only application of not abiding in the doctrine. Denying the inspiration of Scripture would be included (2 Tim. 3:16-17). Denying that repentance is essential to salvation would be included (Acts 17:30-31).

In 1 Corinthians 5, Paul says the church should deal with the case of fornication (vv. 1, 9). The specific application was a man who had his father's wife (v. 1). Surely that is not the only application to be made of that text. What about a case of a woman with her mother's husband?

The same principle is true with 2 Thessalonians 3. Paul uses the general term "disorderly" (v. 6), giving the specific application of not working (vv. 10-11). What about a man who works, but refuses to care for his family? Would that not also be an application of "disorderly"?

Passage	General Principle	Specific Application	Also Would Include
2 John 4-11	Not abiding in doctrine (v. 9)	Denial of Christ (v. 7)	Deny Inspiration Deny Repentance
1 Cor. 5	Fornication (vv. 1, 9)	Man-Father's Wife (v. 1)	Woman-Mother's Husband
2 Thess. 3	Disorderly (v. 6)	Not working (vv. 10-11)	Refuses to care for family

The Purpose of Withdrawing Is not Fulfilled

There is more to withdrawing than a public announcement that the erring is not faithful and is no longer considered a member. Withdrawing involves contact and association beyond the assembly (1 Cor. 5:9, 11; 2 Thess. 3:14). It is possible that one could "withdraw himself" by not assembling and yet desire company and association with the brethren.

Part of the problem is when the term "withdrawing fellowship" is used. While the concept may be scriptural, the expression is not found in the text. The text actually says, "withdraw yourselves" (2 Thess. 3:6). One who has "withdrawn himself" may have removed "fellowship," but withdrawing goes beyond that. We are to remove our person, our company, and our association from the erring (2 Thess. 3:14).

The purpose has not all been fulfilled. One purpose for discipline is seeking to save the erring (1 Cor. 5:5). His quitting does nothing on our part to restore him. Refusing association is to make him ashamed (2 Thess. 3:14). That is not accomplished by his mere quitting.

Another purpose is to maintain the purity of the church (1 Cor. 5:6-7). His absence does not remove the leavening influence of his sin (quitting). His lack of service affects others. When the church takes no action, others may reason that they can do the same.

It Is the Church That Is to Withdraw

The church is told to withdraw from the erring. Paul told the church at Corinth to put away the wicked one (1 Cor. 5:13). Paul told the church at Thessalonica to withdraw themselves (2 Thess. 3:6). Those instructions include something done and said in the assembly (1 Cor. 5:4). They also include withholding social contact (1 Cor. 5:9, 11; 2 Thess. 3:14).

The erring is not instructed to withdraw from the church. When he quits, the church still has its responsibility to fulfill. To say otherwise means that when one quits, our responsibility to him is over.

Parallels

Some have drawn parallels in efforts to show that we cannot withdraw from the withdrawn. For example, some have said if one quits his job, he cannot be fired. So, likewise, when one quits (withdraws himself from the church), the church cannot withdraw from him. We will address those kinds of illustrations in the last section of this lesson. Let's consider some parallels found in the Scriptures.

Israel and Judah. Both the northern and southern kingdoms forgot God (Jer. 2:32; 3:6-10). They left God. They forsook the Lord (Isa. 1:4). Their withdrawal from God did not mean that God would not exercise discipline upon them by allowing Assyrian and Babylonian captivity.

Sheep. The Bible compares God's people to sheep (John 10; Luke 15). The good shepherd goes after his sheep that has gone astray (Luke 15). Elders are compared to shepherds watching over the sheep (Acts 20:28; 1 Pet. 5:1-

4). The responsibility of a shepherd is not removed by the sheep deciding it wants to wander away. To say we cannot withdraw from the "withdrawn" is to say the shepherd cannot go after his sheep.

Note the context connection in Matthew 18 between seeking the straying sheep (vv. 12-14) and corrective discipline (vv. 15-17).

Soldier. The Bible compares a Christian to a soldier (2 Tim. 2:3-4; Eph. 6:10-18; Phil. 2:25). If a solider is AWOL, he is not free of any disciplinary action because he withdrew first!

Creates a Loophole – Can Beat the System

God has a system in place to deal with the disorderly. Simply put, we are to withdraw when one persists in sin (2 Thess. 3:6). Withdrawing includes not socializing with him (2 Thess. 3:14). This is designed to make him ashamed and repent (2 Thess. 3:14).

If we cannot withdraw from one who quits, we have a loophole. All the erring Christian has to do when he sees discipline coming is say, "I quit." That removes all possibility of any discipline on the part of the church.

What is Not Accomplished

Several things are not accomplished by the erring one quitting. Some seem to think that all that could be achieved by withdrawal has been achieved when the erring Christian quits.

The offender does not know that the church has withdrawn from him. Since he is the one that quit or left, he thinks he withdrew from them. If the church does not withdraw, he knows nothing about any disciplinary action toward him.

He does not realize that he has been delivered to Satan (1 Cor. 5:5).

The rest of the church does not know that he has been disciplined. They do not know his leaving accomplished the action of 1 Corinthians 5. They do not know that they should not have company with him (1 Cor. 5:9).

The primary purpose of discipline is not accomplished. The erring one is to be made ashamed of his sin (2 Thess. 3:14). Discipline is done that he might be saved (1 Cor. 5:5). Nothing has been done by his quitting to make him ashamed or bring him to repentance.

His corrupting influence has not been addressed. His example of quitting with no action taken is corrupting. He may continue the social contact, thus a corrupting influence on the faithful.

Questions To Be Answered

Is the one who quits ("withdraws himself") walking disorderly? If he is, should we not withdraw from him (2 Thess. 3:6)? If not, is his action orderly (keeping ranks)?

Can we socialize with one who quits? If not keeping company is designed to bring others to repentance, would not that also be true of one who quits? If we are not to keep company with him, why can we not withdraw from him? If one part of the withdrawing instructions apply to him, why not the rest? If we can socialize with him, why would that not deter his repentance as in the case of the fornicator?

If one quits attending, should something be said to identify him as being in sin? Should something be said to him that he is no longer considered as a faithful member? Should something be said to the church that the erring is no longer considered a member? If he wants to socialize, should we identify his sin and refuse? If you answer yes to the above, what is the difference in that and withdrawing from him? If you answer no to the above, why would you answer "no"?

What if one quits attending and joins a denomination? Does the sin of denominationalism make a difference? Should the church withdraw?

What if a fornicator says, "I withdraw myself" and yet keeps attending? We might ask, "What is left to withdraw?" Does the fact that he has "withdrawn himself" mean that the principles of 1 Corinthians 5 do not come to play?

Arguments Made Against Withdrawing from the Withdrawn

"Those who were to be withdrawn from were still attending because they were 'among you' (1 Cor. 5:1, 2; 2 Thess. 3:11)." There is nothing in these passages that demand a conclusion that the erring Christians were still attending.

The term "among you" is not limited to the assembly. Elders have the oversight of the flock of God "among you" (1 Pet. 5:1-2). This oversight includes all that takes place in the assembly. It also includes activities outside the assembly of the church.

Furthermore, Paul worked night and day "among you" (1 Thess. 2:7, 9; 2 Thess. 3:7-8). This is an obvious reference to secular work that was not in the assembly. "Were they all working on the same job at the same place and time? Impossible to prove. Yet Paul could say he was 'among them' even during the time he was working night and day, though he might not have seen them for days at a time."[2]

"2 Thessalonians 3 only applies to those not working." The term "disorderly" means "*out of the ranks,* (often so of soldiers); ... *deviating from the prescribed order or rule:* 1 Th. 5:14, cf. 2 Th. 3:6.*"*[3] To cite one specific application (as Paul did) does not limit the term to that one sin. If 2 Thessalonians 3 is limited to not working, we must do that same with 1 Corinthians 5—limit the term "fornication" to a man with this father's wife.

"If 'disorderly' is a broad term, then we must withdraw from all who are disorderly (less than perfect)." This argument makes an absurd leap. It is like saying, "If 'disorderly' means those that are not working, then we must withdraw from all who don't work—even those that don't work for one day!"

The truth is: "disorderly" describes one who persists in sin. He "walks disorderly" (v. 6). "Disorderly" describes a manner of life. Furthermore, he refuses to obey the word (v. 14). Consider the Amplified Bible's translation of 2 Thessalonians 3:14, "But if anyone [in the church] refuses to obey what

---

2   Ralph Williams, *Torch,* July 1977, p. 9.
3   Thayer, J. H. (1889). *A Greek-English lexicon of the New Testament: Being Grimm's Wilke's Clavis Novi Testamenti* (p. 83). New York: Harper & Brothers.

we say in this letter, take note of that person and do not associate with him, so that he may be ashamed."

"Yeast can't leaven the lump when it is removed from the lump." This agrument assumes that not assembling has accomplished all that 1 Corinthians 5 was designed to do. There is influence outside the assembly—i.e. keeping company (vv. 9, 11).

"Once one has left, what remains to be withdrawn?" Some give an illustration of 10 dimes, suggesting that you remove one dime from the other nine. Now, try to remove the nine from the one. "It can't be done", we are told.

This argument assumes all that is involved in withdrawal is accomplished by his leaving. It also assumes that there is no other connection between brethren still attending and the one that quit.

Back to the dime illustration, the one dime that was separated might be further separated by spending it and not the rest. The point is, all is not accomplished (that may need to be) by the mere separation of one coin. Likewise, the mere separation of one does not accomplish all that should be accomplished in discipline.

Let's try this argument on for size with a person who will not work. Remember, some tell us we can and should withdraw from him. But, suppose that the one who will not work at all still attends and announces, "I withdraw myself." Would "What else is there to withdraw?" work in this case? Would the dime illustration ("How can you remove the nine from the one?") apply?

Could One Refuse to Be Withdrawn From?

If one who quits attending has "withdrawn himself" (meaning there is nothing more we can do), then if one continues to attend, does that mean that he refuses to be withdrawn from (meaning there is nothing more that we can do)? Ed Bragwell said it best:

> The concept that we cannot withdraw from the withdrawn (meaning one who no longer attends) because he has withdrawn himself presents still another problem. Suppose a brother (or sister) becomes an adulterer but still attends all

services, sings, bows in prayer, eats the Lord's Supper, etc. (we have known this to happen)—can the church withdraw from him?

"Of course, it can," you say.

But wait a minute. Does the fact that he still attends regularly and participates in worship not mean that he refuses to be withdrawn from? How can the church withdraw from one who refuses to be withdrawn from?

"But, we can't keep him from coming and participating," you say.

Right!

"We can announce that we no longer fellowship him."

Right again!

"Each member can refuse to associate with him on a day to day basis."

Right one more time!

"After all, we can 'withdraw ourselves' from him even though he is regular in attendance and participates in the worship."

Now, my brother, you are beginning to get the point! If the fact that one quits means that he has "withdrawn himself" and we cannot withdraw from him then, if one refuses to quit it must mean that there is nothing further we can do, since he refuses to be withdrawn from. If not, why not?

We can mark and refuse to company with a brother who walks disorderly whether or not he attends services. In fact, the very refusal to attend faithfully is walking disorderly and is grounds for marking and withdrawing ourselves.[4]

Questions

1. How do we know that not attending worship services is included in the word "disorderly"? _____
   _____
   _____

2. What are the consequences of saying that the word "disorderly" in 2 Thessalonians 3 only applies to those not working? _____
   _____
   _____

3. Why would we say the purpose of church discipline is not fulfilled when the erring quits? _____
   _____
   _____
   _____

4. What parallels can be drawn from the scriptures that harmonize with withdrawing from the withdrawn? _____
   _____
   _____
   _____

5. What loophole is created if we can't withdraw from those who have withdrawn themselves? _____
   _____
   _____

6. What are some principles of church discipline that are not accomplished by the erring just quitting? _____
   _____
   _____

---

4 From an article, "Can We Withdraw from the Withdrawn?," http://www.edssermonsandthings.com/wp-content/uploads/2016/05/July_15.pdf.

7. How would you answer the contention that those who were to be disciplined were still attending for they were "among you" (1 Cor. 5:1, 2; 2 Thess. 3:11)? _____
_____
_____

8. How would you answer the argument that says 2 Thessalonians 3 only applies to those not working? _____
_____
_____

9. How would you answer the contention that says if "disorderly" involves those not following the rule, then we must withdraw from anyone that is less than perfect? _____
_____
_____
_____

10. How would you answer the argument that says once one has left, there is nothing left to withdraw? _____
_____
_____
_____

Procedure for Withrawal

Lesson 12

The questions to be considered are: How does a church go about withdrawing from an erring brother? Are there certain steps to be followed? Is there a prescribed method to be used? The Bible does not give a specific formula or procedure. However, Christians must follow certain Bible principles.

There is a need to discuss procedure due to the extremes in opinions. One extreme is when someone wants to withdraw the moment we learn of some brother's guilt. Another extreme is withdrawing without even going to the one from whom we are withdrawing. Even another extreme is withdrawing from someone after two years or more of living in sin and twenty or thirty visits.

Let's consider what should be done before the withdrawal, the withdrawal, and what should be done after the withdrawal.

Before the Withdrawal

Establish guilt and the facts. When Jesus addresses personal offenses (Matt. 18:15-17), His instructions show that the charge and the facts are well established before they ever reach "church" level (v. 17). The case of fornication at Corinth was "commonly" (KJV) or "actually" (NKJV) reported (1 Cor. 5:1-2). The word translated "commonly" means "Literally, wholly, altogether, ... So papyri have it for 'really' and also for 'generally' or 'everywhere' as is possible here."[1] Thus, the report is both known and accurate.

The charge should not be based on suspicion or rumor. An accusation against an elder should not be regarded without it being established by

---

1 Robertson, A. T. (1933). *Word Pictures in the New Testament* (1 Cor. 5:1). Nashville, TN: Broadman Press.

two or three witnesses (1 Tim. 5:19). This protects his reputation from a disgruntled member's charges. We must be willing to give the benefit of the doubt when someone's guilt is in question (1 Cor. 13:7; Prov. 18:13, 17). We would want others to give us the benefit of the doubt (Matt. 7:12).

This principle involves treating the brother or sister as innocent until evidence is provided. There have been occasions where a member of the local church has made accusations about another member being guilty of some sin and pleaded that some action be taken, like no longer use the brother in the worship service. However, when pressed for the evidence of the charge, there either was none to give or was unwilling to share it lest it be found that he or she was the one bringing the change. In each of those cases, it was wise to treat the brother who was charged with wrong as innocent until someone could prove that he was guilty.

Ample warnings and pleas. We cannot withdraw the moment we learn of someone's guilt even with abundant evidence. Neither do we withdraw before giving a warning. There are occasions where some sin was learned on a Thursday or Friday, and some brother is ready to announce withdrawal on Sunday—and that without any plea or warning.

It takes time and maybe more than one plea to restore the erring (Gal. 6:1). The instructions on personal offenses demonstrate that we must exhaust efforts to reconcile and gain the brother (Matt. 18:15-17). The unruly[2] should be warned about their condition before God (1 Thess. 5:14).

Paul told Titus that there should be multiple admonitions before rejecting a heretic (Tit. 3:10). In light of this and the above passages, we should not entertain any idea of withdrawing until we have made repeated efforts to restore. Efforts will be rendered useless if there is delay (cf. Eccl. 8:11).

Inform the erring of intent. The instructions of 1 Corinthians 5 and 2 Thessalonians 3 imply that the erring Christian is informed. For example, since withdrawing is designed to produce repentance (1 Cor. 5:5; 2 Thess. 3:14), surely, the erring needs to know about the action of the church toward him. Likewise, since the faithful are not to keep company with the erring (1 Cor. 5:9, 11; 2 Thess. 3:14), surely, the wayward must be informed why that is happening. Otherwise, how effective will it be?

---

2   Unruly is from the same word translated "disorderly" (2 Thess. 3:6).

If the church does not inform the erring Christian concerning the intent to withdraw, the church does not give an opportunity for the erring one to correct his life before they take action.

How we inform him is not specified in the Scriptures. We could notify him orally (personally or by phone). We could use a letter (either hardcopy or electronically).

How much time there should be between informing the one to be disciplined and the withdrawing is a matter of judgment. It might be a week or two weeks later. It may even vary according to the maturity of the one guilty.

The Withdrawal

The manner with which we need to handle the withdrawal. How (the manner and attitude) we handle the act of withdrawing will make all the difference in how effective it will be.

1. *Action taken should be done in a manner to accomplish the objective.* The objective is to gain the brother (Matt. 18:15-17) or save his soul (James 5:20; 1 Cor. 5:5). Church discipline should not be approached like we are going through a checklist to get it done.

2. *Act with the spirit of love and kindness (Rom. 13:10; 1 Cor. 16:14).* All our dealings with the erring should display love and concern. Announcing that we are withdrawing from a brother or sister should display more care than we may show in listing who is leading singing, waiting on the table or is out sick. Any communication with the erring (before or after) should display our love for him.

3. *Use wisdom and judgment (Phil. 1:9-10; Col. 1:9).* These passages show that wisdom and discernment go beyond knowledge. We must use wisdom in how we approach disciplining the erring one. We must use good judgment in how we word our conversations with him. We need some discernment concerning the timing of our actions.

4. *Striving always to follow the law of Christ.* There is a connection between restoring the erring (Gal. 6:1) and following the law of Christ (v. 2). We are always obliged to follow the law of Christ (James 1:25). It should be clear

to the congregation and the one being disciplined that we are doing this because we want to be right with God.

Action in the assembly (1 Cor. 5:4). Paul says the church at Corinth is to deliver the wayward brother to Satan "when you are gathered together." By taking this action in the assembly, the leaders are informing the church. They are letting the church know that there is no longer any fellowship with the erring. This public action marks the point at which the unruly one is delivered unto Satan (1 Cor. 5:5). And, this lets the church know that the relationship with the erring has changed. Now, the plea for repentance is public.

After the Withdrawal

Have no fellowship. Paul writes, "And have no fellowship with the unfruitful works of darkness, but rather expose them" (Eph. 5:11). We cannot have fellowship in any way with the one who has been disciplined until he repents. If he continues to attend, we cannot accept him as a member (cf. Acts 9:26-28) or use him in the services (leading prayer, etc.).

Have no company (1 Cor. 5:9, 11; 2 Thess. 3:14).

Continue to admonish (2 Thess. 3:15). Our responsibility is not over when we announce that we are withdrawing from the erring brother. As a child of God, use any opportunity to make a plea for repentance—not only as we casually run into the brother, but deliberately making efforts to contact him with such pleas.

Remember that time does not erase the situation. Man can quickly forget what happened years ago. However, without repentance, God still remembers (cf. Jude 6). The point is that, after we withdraw from a brother and five, ten, even twenty years pass, time does not change his condition before God and how we should treat him.

Questions

1. Why do we need to discuss procedure when there is no exact procedure or formula given in the Scriptures? _____
   _____
   _____

2. What are three things to be done before the withdrawal? _____
   _____
   _____
   _____

3. How should a brother be treated about whom a rumor or suspicion (but there is no hard evidence) says he is guilty of wrong? _____
   _____
   _____

4. What reason(s) can you give for giving ample warning before withdrawing? _____
   _____
   _____

5. What is the danger of taking too long in giving the erring time to repent? _____
   _____
   _____

6. Why should a church inform the erring of their intent to withdraw? __
   _____
   _____

7. When a church withdraws from a brother, does it have to send a letter?
   _____
   _____
   _____

8. What is the manner in which we should approach the erring to make the discipline effective? _____
_____
_____

9. What should be done in the assembly regarding withdrawing and why?
_____
_____
_____
_____

10. What should be done after the withdrawal? _____
_____
_____
_____

Objections and Questions about Withdrawing

Lesson 13

Despite the clarity of the command to withdraw from the disorderly, there are Christians who oppose it and object to it. Arguments and quibbles are offered to justify their objections. We shall consider some of those in this lesson. Additionally, there are questions often raised about discipline which we seek to answer here as well.

Objections

Objection: "The parable of the wheat and tares (Matt. 13:24-30) suggests that we leave the wayward Christian alone and let the Lord do the separation at the end of time."

No Scripture should be interpreted to contradict another Scripture. This interpretation contradicts 1 Corinthians 5:1-13. This interpretation contradicts 2 Thessalonians 3:6-15.

One finds the Lord's interpretation of the parable in Matthew 13:36-43. The Lord says the "field" in this parable is the "world" (v. 38). It is not the church. In fact, Paul's instructions on church discipline (1 Cor. 5) are not talking about separating from the sinners of the world (v. 10). This parable has no application to church discipline.

Objection: "It doesn't do any good. It just drives people away."

Consider a parallel. Suppose someone said, "Preaching the gospel doesn't do any good. It just drives people away." Preaching does not convert all, but it does convert some. On the other hand, preaching does drive some away. Yet, we do not stop preaching the gospel. The same is true concerning church discipline. It does not cause all to repent, but it does cause some to have a change of heart. Withdrawing worked at Corinth. It brought the erring brother back (2 Cor. 2). When we obey God's commands, good is done. If nothing else is accomplished, we have at least obeyed God.

If withdrawing is not doing any good, it may be that the church is not exercising the discipline as it should. It may not be doing it as the text requires. It may not be in the manner or spirit we should have. Withdrawing is much like exercising discipline upon our children (Prov. 22:15). When a parent says that he has disciplined his child, but it does not do any good, he probably is being inconsistent or not applying it as he should. This does not mean that discipline does not work in either case.

If one is walking disorderly, he is already "away" from God. Discipline is not going to drive him away. It is designed to bring him back (1 Cor. 5:5).

Objection: "We are not to judge (Matt. 7:1). Withdrawing involves judging."

The context of Matthew 7 deals with hypocrisy. Jesus does not condemn judging in this passage. Judging another while guilty of the same or worse is condemned (vv. 3-4). In fact, we are told to remove the plank from our own eye, then help remove the speck from the brother's eye (v. 5). That involves judging.

We are to judge. We have to judge whether one is a false teacher to beware of him (Matt. 7:15). Jesus said we should judge with righteous judgment (John 7:24). Paul said that church discipline does and should involve some judging (1 Cor. 5:12-13).

It seems inconsistent to use a passage that says not to judge, to judge us for judging.

Objection: "We didn't withdraw from _____. So, how can we withdraw from anyone else?"

In Nehemiah 8, post-exile Israel learned that they were not observing the Feast of Tabernacles as they should (by dwelling in booths). So, they started dwelling in booths (v. 17). They did not argue, "We didn't do that last year, so why do it this year?"

How long should this procrastination continue? Do we never practice discipline if we failed to do so in a previous case?

This would mean that any failure justifies a continual failure to obey God. If we fail to observe the Lord's Supper, we cannot start now because "We didn't observe it last week." If we fail to have qualified elders, we cannot start now because "We didn't have qualified elders before." If we fail to meet on the Lord's day, we cannot start now because "We didn't do that last year."

Objection: "We all sin. So, why single out one member and withdraw from him?"

Yes, we all do sin (1 John 1:8). However, all do not practice sin (1 John 3:6, 9; Rom. 6). All are not disorderly ("unruly," 1 Thess. 5:14). At Corinth, all the members sinned, but all were not fornicators (1 Cor. 5). At Thessalonica, all the members sinned, but all were not lazy (2 Thess. 3).

Objection: "What does the world think when they see how we treat one of our members?"

This objection is more concerned about what the world or the community thinks than what God thinks. We should be concerned what the world or community thinks if we do not take disciplinary action.

There have been non-Christians who have been attracted to the gospel and the church because a congregation took action against sin.

In Lesson 5 there was mention of a young lady having a home bible study with a member of the church. She attended worship services on the day when the elders announced the congregation was withdrawing from five of its members. Being supportive of the elders' decision, this action had the possibility of creating questions of doubt or terminating the Bible study altogether. However, at the next study she was excited to learn there was a church which took a stand and dealt with sin. She said they did not do that where she had previously attended. What she had seen concerning discipline in a congregation actually impressed her.

The church that is clean and does not tolerate sin is the best advertisement a church can have (cf. Rom. 2:23-24).

Objection: "Trying to withdraw from people will tear up this church."

Doing what the Lord commands (2 Thess. 3:6) will not tear up a church. It did not tear up the church at Corinth at all (2 Cor. 2). In fact, not dealing with sin was going to tear it up (1 Cor. 5:6-7). A church that does not practice discipline is in shambles anyway.

Questions about Withdrawing

Question: "What about the wayward Christian who was not withdrawn from (though he should have been)—should we not socialize or personally withdraw from him?"

This situation could come in several scenarios: One who is faithful moves away and places membership in another church in another city or state. Then, he becomes unfaithful. The church there does not withdraw. Then the unfaithful Christian comes back into the area of the first church where he was once faithful. Can the members of that church socialize with him? Should they personally withdraw themselves from him?

Another scenario might be a family member or good friend who worships with a church that does not practice discipline. The family member or friend becomes unfaithful (but was not withdrawn from by that church). Can I continue to associate with him? Should I not keep company with him to bring him to repentance?

There is a principle of how to treat the erring to win him back to the Lord which involves not keeping company with him (1 Cor. 5:9, 11; 2 Thess. 3:14). The church where the erring was not a member is not responsible for the withdrawal. Individually, each can and should practice "not keeping company" with the erring. To do otherwise would seem to work against the efforts to reach the erring one. To think that socializing (keeping company) will help win them back contradicts the text.

Question: "Can one church withdraw from another church?"

There is no command, example, or inference of such in the New Testament. No church was ever instructed to withdraw from another congregation. There is no record of one church withdrawing from another church.

We must recognize the difference in the individual and the church (1 Tim. 5:16). The church at Corinth withdrew from an individual (1 Cor. 5). The church at Thessalonica withdrew from individuals (2 Thess. 3).

We are made to wonder how this practice works. Within what radius does this work? Does this only apply to a church within 20 miles or would it include those within 200 miles or even 2000 miles? How would a church determine where that limit is? We also wonder if one church could withdraw from a member of another church? If one church can withdraw from another church, why could not that same church withdraw from a member in that second church?

A second church is not under the oversight of the elders of the first church (1 Pet. 5:1-2). However, the elders could warn the church where they are the leaders about the dangerous practices of another congregation or an individual (i.e. a preacher teaching error) that might influence those members (cf. Rom. 6:17).

Question: "Is one congregation bound to accept the withdrawal that took place in another congregation?"

No. Each person or situation would have to be accepted or rejected on its merit (cf. Acts 9:26-28). Each church is autonomous and independent (Acts 20:28; 1 Pet. 5:1-4). Thus, one church is not bound by what another does.

It is possible for a church to be wrong in their action of withdrawing. They may have withdrawn without sufficient evidence. They may have withdrawn for the wrong reason. For example, a church may withdraw from a brother and label him as a troublemaker for opposing a false teacher within the church.

This does not mean that we simply ignore what another church has done. Wise elders should gather all the facts before accepting or rejecting one who has been disciplined (cf. Acts 9:26-28; Prov. 18:13, 17).

Question: "If a church has not been practicing discipline in the past, but wants to begin now, how far back should they go in withdrawing from unfaithful members?"

A church has to start where they are. The past cannot be undone, so the church needs to repent of the failures in the past. A congregation can repent and change (Rev. 2:1-7).

A church cannot go back and discipline those who have been gone for years (i.e. those who have moved away or are now dead, etc.). If there are disorderly members in the church at the present, that is where a church must start. We cannot fail to obey a command because it is hard to figure out where to start.

As noted in lesson 7, there was a congregation that had not practiced discipline in thirty years. After a series of lessons on church discipline, the elders made a public confession and statement about the matter. Their public statement was something like the following:

> As elders of this church we are not responsible for the failure to exercise discipline for the past thirty years, but we are responsible for the time that we have been elders. We acknowledge our sin in not leading the church in this matter. We ask God and you to forgive us of this wrong. We cannot go back and undo the past. We cannot go back and withdraw from someone who should have been disciplined years ago. However, we can start where we are now. There are some in this church who are walking disorderly. We plan to do what is right and withdraw from them.

Question: "What are the legal implications of withdrawing? How can a church avoid a lawsuit over discipline? Could a church decide not to withdraw if the elders are afraid of a lawsuit?"

There have been several cases of lawsuits over church discipline among churches of Christ starting in the mid-1980's. The most notable case was the church in Collinsville, OK. The case (Guinn v. church of Christ of Collinsville) went all the way to the state supreme court.

We cannot afford to let fear keep us from following God's word. We should have a greater fear of judgment (2 Cor. 5:10). Should we accept someone practicing homosexuality lest he sue us for not accepting him? Should we allow a woman to preach lest she sue us for discrimination?

Following some simple principles may prevent a lawsuit (or at least keep one from going anywhere). Several years ago when the church where I preached was under the threat of a lawsuit over church discipline, I sought some advice from a preacher who was also an attorney. He served as a judge and was also appointed to the Tennessee Court of Appeals. Additionally, he was in the court room in most (if not all) of the cases of churches of Christ being sued in the 1980's and 1990's (not as a defense attorney, but in an advisory role).

He suggested that a church that wants to avoid a lawsuit do two things: (1) *Be consistent.* Do not withdraw from one person for adultery, while others are guilty of the same. (2) *Be sure you have the evidence or proof.* Do not try to "pile on" the reasons for withdrawing. A church only needs one reason. For example, if you have evidence of one sin, but also pretty sure there are other sins (but cannot prove it), only mention the one sin that can be proven.

When we do what we should, we will follow these rules.

Hopefully, these thirteen lessons on church discipline have helped us get a better understanding of the Lord's instructions on the subject. Church discipline is an effort at saving the erring, saving the church, saving our families, and saving ourselves.

Questions

1. Using the parable of the wheat and tares (Matt. 13:24-30), how can you show it is a misapplication to apply this parable as an argument against church discipline? _____
_____
_____
_____

2. How would you respond to the charge that discipline does not do any good, it just drives people away? _____
_____
_____

3. How can we withdraw from a brother without being guilty of judging (Matt. 7:1)? _____
_____
_____

4. How would you answer the statement, "We all sin. So why single out one member and withdraw from him?" _____
_____
_____

5. How should one be treated who is a wayward Christian, but a church has not withdrawn from him (though it should have)? _____
_____
_____

6. Can one church withdraw from another church? Explain. _____
_____
_____
_____

7. Is one congregation bound to accept the withdrawal that took place in another congregation? _____
_____
_____

8. What should a church do that has not been practicing discipline but wants to now? _____
_____
_____

9. How can a church avoid legal trouble over withdrawing? _____
   _____
   _____
   _____

10. What has stood out most for you in this series of studies? _____
    _____
    _____
    _____
    _____

www.ingramcontent.com/pod-product-compliance
Lightning Source LLC
Chambersburg PA
CBHW070450050426
42451CB00015B/3415